Teacher's Guide

PATHWAYS

Listening, Speaking, and Critical Thinking

FOUNDATIONS

Ingrid Wisniewska

 NATIONAL GEOGRAPHIC LEARNING |  HEINLE CENGAGE Learning·

Australia • Brazil • Japan • Korea • Mexico • Singapore • Spain • United Kingdom • United States

Pathways Foundations Teacher's Guide
Listening, Speaking, and Critical Thinking
Ingrid Wisniewska

Publisher: Sherrise Roehr

Executive Editor: Laura Le Dréan

Development Editor: Katherine Carroll

Director of Global Marketing: Ian Martin

Marketing Manager: Caitlin Thomas

Marketing Manager: Emily Stewart

Director of Content and Media Production: Michael Burggren

Senior Content Project Manager: Daisy Sosa

Manufacturing Manager: Marcia Locke

Manufacturing Buyer: Marybeth Hennebury

Cover Design: Page 2 LLC

Cover Image: Denis Burdin/Shutterstock

Interior Design: Page 2 LLC, Cenveo Publisher Services®/Nesbitt Graphics, Inc.

Composition: Cenveo Publisher Services

ISBN-13: 978-1-285-17627-7

ISBN-10: 1-285-17627-8

National Geographic Learning
20 Channel Center St.
Boston, MA 02210
USA

Cengage Learning is a leading provider of customized learning solutions with office locations around the globe, including Singapore, the United Kingdom, Australia, Mexico, Brazil, and Japan. Locate your local office at: **international.cengage.com/region**

Cengage Learning products are represented in Canada by Nelson Education, Ltd.

Visit National Geographic Learning online at **www.ngl.cengage.com**
Visit our corporate website at **www.cengage.com**

Printed in the United States of America
1 2 3 4 5   17 16 15 14 13

TABLE OF CONTENTS

Advantages of *Pathways Listening, Speaking, and Critical Thinking*

In *Pathways Listening, Speaking, and Critical Thinking*, real-world content from *National Geographic* publications provides a context for meaningful language acquisition. Students learn essential, high-frequency vocabulary, review important grammatical structures, and practice listening and speaking skills that will allow them to succeed in both academic and social settings.

Pathways Listening, Speaking, and Critical Thinking can be used in a wide variety of language-learning programs, from high schools and community colleges to private institutes and intensive English programs. The high-interest content motivates students and teachers alike.

The following features are included in *Pathways Listening, Speaking, and Critical Thinking*:

- Academic Pathways give students and teachers clear performance objectives for each unit.

- Opening pages introduce the unit theme and provide key vocabulary and concepts.

- Interesting content is used to present target vocabulary and to spark discussions.

- Extensive audio programs include lectures, interviews, conversations, and pronunciation models that expose students to many different kinds of speakers.

- Clear grammar charts present key grammar structures and explain language functions such as asking for clarification and sustaining a conversation.

- Presentation Skills boxes highlight skills for planning and delivering successful oral presentations.

- Student to Student boxes provide real-world expressions for making friends and working with classmates.

- An *Independent Student Handbook* and vocabulary index at the end of each level serve as tools to use in class or for self-study and review.

Teaching Language Skills and Academic Literacy

Students need more than language skills to succeed in an academic setting. In addition to teaching the English language, the *Pathways* series teaches academic literacy, which includes not only reading, writing, speaking, and listening skills, but also visual literacy, classroom participation and collaboration skills, critical thinking, and the ability to use technology for learning. Students today are expected to be motivated, inquisitive, original, and creative. In short, they're expected to possess quite an extensive skill set before they even begin their major course of study.

Using *National Geographic* Content in a Language Class

The use of high-interest content from *National Geographic* publications sets the *Pathways* series apart. Instead of working with topics that might seem irrelevant, students are engaged by fascinating stories about real people and places around the world and the issues that affect us all.

High-interest content is introduced throughout each unit—as context for target vocabulary, as content for lectures and conversation—and provides the information students need for lively discussions and interesting presentations.

The topics in the *Pathways Listening, Speaking, and Critical Thinking* series correspond to academic subject areas and appeal to a wide range of interests. For example:

Academic Subject Area	Unit Title	Unit Theme
Sociology/Psychology	*Taking Risks*	risk-taking, danger, physical activities, and reactions to them; self-evaluation of adventurousness
History/Anthropology/Archaeology	*Lost and Found*	ancient civilizations and the lessons they impart about the value of history
Anthropology/Sociology	*Same and Different*	population and family trends around the world; similarities and differences between individuals; coming of age customs
Interdisciplinary	*Enjoy the Ride!*	ways of traveling and means of transportation
Science/Technology	*A New View*	current and possible future technology, including robots, bionics, cloning; technology in daily life, agriculture, medicine

Increasing Visual Literacy

Photographs, maps, charts, and graphs can all convey enormous amounts of information. Lecturers and professors rarely give oral presentations without some kind of visual aid. Helping students to make sense of visuals is an important part of preparing them for academic success.

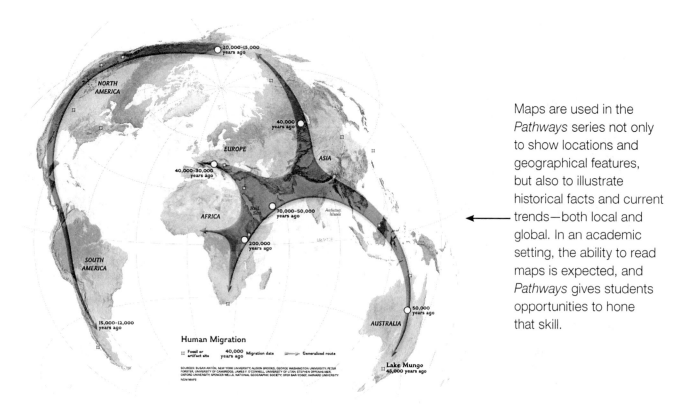

Maps are used in the *Pathways* series not only to show locations and geographical features, but also to illustrate historical facts and current trends—both local and global. In an academic setting, the ability to read maps is expected, and *Pathways* gives students opportunities to hone that skill.

v

Charts and graphs present numerical data in a visual way, and the *Pathways* series gives students practice in reading them. In addition to the standard pie charts and bar graphs, *Pathways* includes more unusual visuals from the pages of *National Geographic* publications.

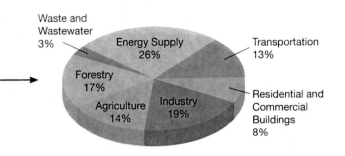

Waste and Wastewater 3%

Energy Supply 26%

Transportation 13%

Forestry 17%

Agriculture 14%

Industry 19%

Residential and Commercial Buildings 8%

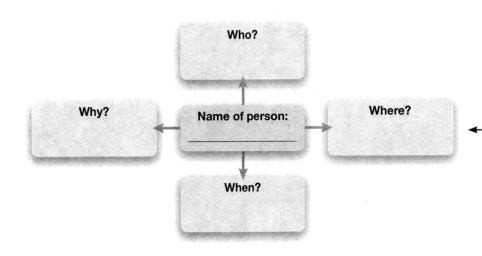

Who?

Why?

Name of person:

Where?

When?

Graphic organizers have several functions in the *Pathways* series. They appeal to visual learners by showing relationships between ideas in a visual way. So, in addition to texts and listening passages, *Pathways* uses graphic organizers to present interesting content. Students are asked to use graphic organizers for a number of academic tasks such as generating topics or organizing notes for a presentation.

The photographs in the *Pathways* series go far beyond decorating the pages. Photographs introduce the unit theme and provide necessary background information for understanding listening passages and texts. Teachers will also want to exploit the photographs in *Pathways* to initiate discussions and reinforce the target language.

Building Critical Thinking Skills

Critical thinking skills are explicitly taught and practiced in *Pathways Listening, Speaking, and Critical Thinking.* One reason for this is that critical thinking—the ability to make judgments and decisions based on evidence and reason—is an essential skill for students in an academic setting, where they're expected to reflect on and analyze information rather than simply remember it. Students need to be prepared to think critically while listening, reading, writing, and participating in discussions. The skills of critical thinking do not develop on their own; they need to be taught, learned, and practiced.

The ability to think critically is also required in most careers, and critical thinking contributes to language acquisition by requiring deep processing of the language. In order to consider an idea in relation to other ideas and then articulate a response or an opinion about it, we must make complex associations in the brain. This in turn leads to better comprehension and retention of the target language.

Here are just a few examples of the academic tasks that require critical thinking skills:

- deciding which material from a lecture to take notes on

- determining a speaker's purpose when assessing the content of a talk

- forming an opinion on an issue based on facts and evidence

- relating new information to one's personal experiences

- giving specific examples to support one's main idea

- assessing the credibility of a source of information

The *Pathways* series gives explicit instruction on and practice of critical thinking skills. Each unit has a Critical Thinking Focus and several practice exercises. For example:

Critical Thinking Focus: Drawing Conclusions

When you draw a conclusion, you make a logical judgment about something based on the information you have. For example, *I might stop by your house. If there are no lights on, and when I knock on the door nobody answers, I'll probably conclude that nobody is home. I can't know this for certain since I can't go into the house and look around, but I do have enough information to reach a logical conclusion.*

 A | In a group, discuss the information from this unit about Angkor and the Khmer Empire and list some conclusions you can draw based on this information. Consider the topics below.

- The length of time that Angkor was the capital of the Khmer Empire
- The art and architecture that can be seen at Angkor
- The number of temples built at Angkor
- The size and sophistication of the water control systems in and around Angkor

> We can conclude that there were a lot of workers in Angkor. Somebody had to construct those huge man-made lakes.

- The fact that Angkor's wealth and power declined after losing river access to the sea
- The fact that Angkor Wat is on UNESCO's World Heritage site list

Teaching with *Pathways Listening, Speaking, and Critical Thinking*

Using the Opening Pages

Each unit of *Pathways Listening, Speaking, and Critical Thinking* begins with a unit opener and a two-page section called Exploring the Theme. These opening pages serve the important function of raising student interest in the unit theme and introducing key vocabulary and concepts.

The Unit Opener

Every unit opener features a stunning photograph that draws students into the unit theme. You'll want to direct students' attention to the photograph and the unit title. Give students a chance to react to the photograph and give the class some of the background information that you'll find in the Teacher's Guide.

Every unit opener also includes Think and Discuss questions that encourage students to interact with the photograph and to relate it to their own lives.

The unit opener also lists the Academic Pathways for each unit. These are clearly stated performance objectives that preview some of the main culminating activities in the unit. The Academic Pathways are also useful in assessing students' progress at the end of each unit.

Exploring the Theme

After you've worked with the unit opener, go on to the two-page Exploring the Theme section, which provides information in the form of maps, captioned photographs, charts and graphs, and short articles. This section gives students the background information and key terms they need before beginning the unit.

The Exploring the Theme questions check students' comprehension of the information and give them a chance to respond to it in a meaningful way.

Building Vocabulary

Each level of *Pathways Listening, Speaking, and Critical Thinking* contains approximately 200 target vocabulary words in addition to footnotes for less frequently used words. The target vocabulary words in the *Pathways* series are . . .

- **High-frequency:** Students are likely to use high-frequency words on a regular basis, which leads to greater acquisition and better fluency.

- **Level-appropriate:** The target vocabulary words in each level of the *Pathways* series are appropriate for the students studying in that level.

- **Useful for discussing the unit theme:** The vocabulary words in each unit are introduced in the vocabulary sections, used in the listening passages, and recycled in many of the activities.

- **Informed by the Academic Word List:** The *Pathways* series contains a high percentage of the words found on the Academic Word List.*

*The Academic Word List (AWL) is a list of the 570 highest-frequency academic word families that regularly appear in academic texts. The AWL was compiled by researcher Averil Coxhead based on her analysis of a 3.5-million-word corpus (Coxhead, 2000).

Developing Listening Skills

Each unit of *Pathways Listening, Speaking, and Critical Thinking* contains two listening sections. The listening passage in Lesson A takes place in a relatively formal context such as a lecture, a meeting, or a formal presentation. Lesson B presents an informal speaking situation such as a conversation between friends or a group project with classmates.

The language in the listening passages represents realistic situations, yet the language is controlled for level, and students may listen to each passage more than once. This guided listening gives students the chance to practice listening and note-taking skills and to develop the confidence and fluency they'll need before they are immersed in an academic setting.

Each listening section contains three parts:

- **Before Listening** activities provide background information and explicit instruction in listening skills.
- **While Listening** activities give students practice in listening for main ideas and smaller details and in making inferences.
- **After Listening** activities are designed to reinforce listening skills and to allow students to discuss and react to the listening passage.

Pronunciation

The pronunciation lessons are designed to increase students' listening comprehension as well as the comprehensibility of their own speech. The focus is on supra-segmentals, such as rhythm and intonation patterns, rather than on individual sounds.

Note-Taking

Pathways Listening, Speaking, and Critical Thinking takes a scaffolding approach to building note-taking skills. Students begin by listening for specific information to fill in blanks. Later they complete partial notes and practice independent note-taking.

Listening Critically

Since critical thinking is an essential part of listening, skills such as identifying a speaker's purpose and summarizing the main points from a talk are part of the *Pathways* listening program.

Listening Homework

Extensive listening can play an important role in increasing listening comprehension. Students can expand on the listening they do in class by using the Audio CD, the Online Workbook, and the Presentation Tool CD-ROM.

Developing Speaking Skills

Every section of *Pathways Listening, Speaking, and Critical Thinking* provides opportunities for classroom speaking and discussion, often in pairs or in small groups. The Exploring Spoken English sections focus entirely on speaking. Striking images and brief stories about real people and places often provide the content for engaging interactions.

Accurate Speech

Clear and succinct grammar lessons give students a single language structure to concentrate on for each Exploring Spoken English section. The grammar points lend themselves to discussion of the unit theme and can be recycled throughout the unit.

Fluent Speech

Frequent classroom discussions and interactions prepare students to participate in class and succeed in an academic setting. Language Function boxes address the situations in which stock expressions or target grammatical structures are commonly used, increasing the students' level of comfort and confidence in dealing with common speaking situations.

Speaking activities are designed with a scaffolding approach. They progress from controlled activities and guided activities to free activities. Early confidence-building motivates students to attempt activities that increase in difficulty, taking them to their ultimate goal—participation in authentic speaking activities such as classroom presentations, formal discussions, and debates.

Presentation Skills boxes appear at points where students give presentations, so they provide immediate practice of skills needed for planning and delivering successful oral presentations.

Student to Student boxes provide tips and expressions to help students develop the informal, one-on-one speaking skills they will need for class work and in their day-to-day exchanges.

Engage is a consolidating speaking activity. It is a task or project involving collaboration with a partner or a group as well as an oral presentation of results or ideas.

Using Videos in the Language Classroom

The video clips in *Pathways Listening, Speaking, and Critical Thinking* come from the award-winning *National Geographic* film collection and act as a bridge between Lesson A and Lesson B of each unit. The videos consolidate content and skills from Lesson A and illustrate a specific aspect of the unit theme in a visually dynamic way.

What is the Lesson A and B Viewing section?

The viewing section features a video on a theme related to the whole unit. All video clips are on the Online Workbook and the Presentation Tool CD-ROM, as well as on the classroom DVD.

Why teach video-viewing skills?

In daily life, non-fiction videos can be found on television, on the Internet, and in movie theaters in the form of documentaries. Just as *Pathways* provides a wide variety of listening passages to build students' listening skills, the series also builds viewing skills with videos from *National Geographic*. *Pathways* promotes visual and digital literacy so learners can competently use a wide range of modern media.

Videos differ from listening texts in important ways. First, students are processing information by viewing and listening simultaneously. Visual images include information about the video's setting as well as clues found in non-verbal communication, such as facial expressions and body movements. The video may also include animated maps and diagrams to explain information and processes. The soundtrack contains narration, conversations, music, and sound effects. Some contextual words may appear on screen in signs or as identification of people or settings. In addition, full English subtitles (closed captions) are available as a teaching and learning option.

What are the stages of viewing?

Before Viewing prepares students for the video, engages their background knowledge about the topic, and creates interest in what they will watch. Effective ways of previewing include:

■ brainstorming ideas and discussing what the class already knows about the topic;

■ using photographs and the video's title to predict the content;

■ pre-teaching key vocabulary essential to understanding the video content;

■ and skimming the summary reading.

While Viewing may occur multiple times and at different speeds while:

- picking out and understanding the main ideas of the video;

- watching and listening closely for detail;

- and watching and listening for opinion and inference.

After Viewing activities include:

- describing the main points and the sequence of events in the video;

- completing the cloze summary with provided target vocabulary;

- and answering discussion questions that relate the video to the students' own lives or experiences.

How should teachers use the videos to teach?

The narration on each video has been carefully graded to feature vocabulary items and structures that are appropriate for students' proficiency level. Here are techniques for using video in class:

- Have students preview the video by reading the transcript or the summary paragraph.

- Pause, rewind, or fast-forward the video to focus on key segments or events.

- Pause the video midway to allow students to predict what will happen next. Resume the video so students can check their predictions.

- Have students watch the video with the sound off so they can focus on what they see. If this approach is used, follow-up discussion helps students share their ideas about the content of the video. Then play the video with the sound on for students to check their ideas.

- Have students watch without subtitles after which they discuss what they hear; then play with subtitles for students to check their ideas.

- Have students follow the script as they listen to the video to help with intonation, pitch, and stress. Stop and replay key phrases for students to repeat.

- Have students watch the video independently and complete the comprehension questions on the Online Workbook.

- To extend viewing skills to speaking and writing skills, have students make a presentation or create a written report about a short video of their choice, using language they have learned from the Student Book and video narration.

All video scripts are printed at the back of the Teacher's Guide. Teachers have flexibility in how or whether they want students to use the scripts. See individual units in this Teacher's Guide for specific teaching suggestions for each video.

Features of the *Pathways* Teacher's Guide

The *Pathways* Teacher's Guide contains teaching notes, answer keys, and the audio and video scripts. There are also warm-up activities to help teachers present the material in the textbook and overviews of the unit theme and the video clip to help turn teachers into "instant experts."

Academic Pathways Boxes

Each unit in the Teacher's Guide begins with a preview of the Academic Pathways. A description of each pathway is then given at the point where it occurs in the unit along with helpful information for the teacher. Teachers are also directed to the online and the Assessment CD-ROM with Exam*View*® resources that will help to reinforce and assess the skills learned for each pathway.

Ideas for... Boxes

Throughout the *Pathways* Teacher's Guide, you will find boxes with ideas to help both novice and experienced teachers. There are four types of *Ideas for...* boxes:

- **Ideas for Presenting Grammar** boxes provide a variety of ways to introduce grammatical structures and utilize the grammar charts.

- **Ideas for Checking Comprehension** boxes remind teachers of the need to continually assess students' comprehension during every class session.

- **Ideas for Expansion** boxes suggest ways to expand on the content of the book when students need extra instruction or when they have a high level of interest in a topic.

- **Ideas for Multi-level Classes** boxes provide techniques to use in mixed-ability classrooms, where learner diversity can benefit everyone in the class. On the other hand, providing the right kind of help for all the students in any classroom can be a balancing act. When different types of instruction are needed for different learners, teachers must be careful not to embarrass lower-level learners in any way or detract from the learning experience of higher-level learners.

Tips

Tips for instruction and classroom management are provided throughout the *Pathways* Teacher's Guide. The tips are especially helpful to less-experienced teachers, but they are also a resource for more experienced teachers, providing new ideas and adding variety to the classroom routine.

Same and Different

Academic Pathways

Lesson A:	Listening to a Lecture
	Conducting a Survey
Lesson B:	Listening to a Conversation
	Giving a Presentation about Yourself

Unit Theme

Unit 1 explores the topic of personal and cultural identity. What makes us the same, and what makes us different or unique?

Think and Discuss *(page 1)*

5 mins

- Ask students to describe the photo. Point out the unit title and ask how it relates to the photo.

- Discuss question 1 and list ways that twins can be similar: physical characteristics, voice, personality, behavior, talents and abilities, likes and dislikes, and so on. You may want to introduce the term *identical twins*, for twins that look exactly alike.

- Discuss question 2 and encourage students to talk about their own experiences.

- For question 3, brainstorm a list of personal qualities that they think everyone has. For example, *imagination, creativity, kindness, generosity.* This may lead to some interesting disagreement and discussion.

Exploring the Theme

15 mins

(pages 2–3)

The opening spread features a map of the world showing the amount of population growth between 1960 and 2011.

- Go over the information in the key and check that students understand the meaning of the different colors.

- Ask which country's population grew the most during this time period. (Countries that are colored dark orange on the map, such as some parts of Africa.)

- Ask which country's population grew the least during this time period. (Countries that are colored gray on the map, such as Europe, Russia, and Japan.)

- Ask if any information in the map surprises them.

- Discuss the possible reasons for different rates of population growth. For example, access to contraception, education, social support, and also cultural attitudes and religion.

- Ask questions about some of the facts written on the map. For example: *What do we know about Côte d'Ivoire?*

- Discuss question 1. Compare different types of maps. For example, physical maps (that show mountains, rivers, lakes), political maps (that show boundaries between nations) and climate maps (that show rainfall and average temperatures in different regions).

- Discuss question 2. Ask if students can suggest any explanations for why some countries have more population growth than others.

- Ask students to look at the photos and describe them. Discuss question 3.

- Discuss question 4 and lead into a general discussion of cultural differences in families.

IDEAS FOR ... Expansion

Discuss the positive and negative aspects of having a large family. You may want to have students work in groups to come up with a list of reasons for and against having a large family. Then bring groups together and summarize the main points on the board.

If appropriate, discuss cultural differences in families. For example, is it usual to leave home when you marry or become an adult, or to live with or near your extended family? What are the reasons for this? How are families in the U.S. similar to or different from families in other cultures? Are there differences in attitudes to the family between cultural groups in the U.S.?

Building Vocabulary

(page 4)

30 mins

WARM-UP

The Lesson A target vocabulary is presented in the context of children who have grown up in more than one culture.

■ Ask students to say one or two sentences about their culture.

■ Ask if any students feel they belong to more than one culture.

Exercise A.

track 1-01

■ Play the audio so the students can hear the pronunciation.

■ Ask students to read the words aloud.

■ If appropriate, ask them to explain the words they know to their partner.

■ Play the audio again and ask students to repeat.

 ### Exercise B. | Meaning from Context

track 1-02

■ Play the audio while students read.

■ Tell students to pay special attention to the words in blue.

Exercise C. | Using a Dictionary

■ Tell students to use their dictionaries to check any unfamiliar words.

■ Allow time for students to complete their answers individually.

■ Check the answers by saying the first part of each answer and asking students to complete the sentence. For example,

   T: *A carefree person is someone . . .*

   S: *. . . without any problems or worries.*

■ Model the correct pronunciation of any difficult words, or play the audio from exercise A.

■ As a follow-up, ask students to make sentences about themselves using these words.

Answer Key

1. f **2.** a **3.** g **4.** c **5.** h **6.** b **7.** e **8.** d

Note: Students may not be familiar with the game of cricket. Refer them to the gloss and the photo on the next page. Explain that baseball is popular in the U.S. and in Japan, but cricket is popular in the U.K., Australia, India, Pakistan, Sri Lanka, and South Africa.

IDEAS FOR . . . Checking Comprehension

Ask students to say how these two teenagers are similar or different. For example:

Similar: They are both teenagers. They have lived in different cultures. They have traveled to different countries. They speak several languages.

Different: Marisa was born in the U.S., but Toshio was born in Japan. Marisa likes music and movies, but Toshio likes sports.

 # Using Vocabulary *(page 5)*

30 mins

Exercise A.

■ Do the first item as an example.

■ Allow time for students to complete their answers in pairs.

■ Monitor students as they practice the conversations.

■ Give tips on pronunciation and intonation.

■ Ask two volunteers to present their conversation for the class.

■ Ask if any students can describe the differences between baseball and cricket.

Answer Key

1. a native of **2.** home country **3.** foreign **4.** traveler **5.** international **6.** athlete

> TIP   As an extension, tell students to make up their own conversations in pairs, using as many of these words as possible. They can write the conversation for homework.

Exercise B. | Discussion

■ Put students into pairs.

■ Allow time for students to discuss their answers.

■ Ask volunteers to summarize their answers for each question and present them to the class.

■ As a follow-up, make a list on the board of which sports or free time activities are popular in your students' countries (or other countries they know well).

> TIP   At the beginning of a course, it's important for students to get to know each other and become comfortable speaking English together. Use a variety of ways to assign partners and form small groups so that students are not always working with the same people.

Developing Listening Skills *(pages 6-7)*

45 mins

Pronunciation: Word Stress

track 1-03

Explain that word stress means that some words in a sentence are louder and stronger than others.

Exercise A.

track 1-04

Play the audio while students read.

> **IDEAS FOR . . . Presenting Grammar**
>
> Give some additional examples of how to use the word *both*. Write two columns on the board with information about you and another person (e.g., your sister or brother). Use the chart to make sentences using the word *both*. Explain that *both* <u>follows</u> the verb *be*, but goes <u>before</u> other verbs.
>
> Examples: *We are both good cooks. We both play the guitar.*

Exercise B.

- Demonstrate the activity by modeling some questions and answers with a volunteer. Ask a few questions such as, *Do you like sports? Do you listen to music?* until you find two things that are the same and two that are different. Then make sentences as in the example.

- As a follow-up, ask volunteer pairs to say a couple of sentences about themselves. Then ask volunteers from the rest of the class to use the information to make sentences using *and, but,* and *both*.

Before Listening

Exercise A. | Using a Dictionary

Practice the pronunciation of these words.

> **IDEAS FOR . . . Expansion**
>
> Use this opportunity to find out how many students have a monolingual dictionary. Explain the advantages of such a dictionary. Bring an appropriate-level dictionary to class as an example.
>
> Explain that such dictionaries are excellent learning aids because they include synonyms, antonyms, grammar explanations, and example phrases and sentences. Also point out that it can be very misleading to rely on literal translation of words from a bilingual dictionary, as a word can have many different meanings depending on the context.

Exercise B.

- Tell students to write their answers individually.
- Students can compare answers with a partner.

> **Answer Key**
>
> 1. similar 2. shy 3. nervous 4. adopt 5. identical

Exercise C. | Predicting Content

- Emphasize that there is no right or wrong answer at this stage.

- Ask students to explain why it is important to predict content before listening. (It helps you to get your mind ready to receive the new information. It organizes the information you already have on this topic so that you are ready to add new information to it.)

Listening: A Lecture

Exercise A. | Checking Predictions

track 1-05

Do a quick survey of the class to find out which predictions were correct.

Exercise B. | Listening for the Main Idea

track 1-05

Compare answers as a class.

> **Answer Key**
>
> The following main idea should be checked: Some identical twins are similar, and some are very different.

Exercise C. | Listening for Details

track 1-05

Play the audio again and compare answers as a class.

> **Answer Key**
>
> The following facts should be underlined:
>
> <u>1. The two boys lived with different families.</u>
> <u>3. Their wives were named Linda and Betty.</u>
> <u>7. They both had sons named James Alan.</u>
> <u>8. They are 39 years old now.</u>

> **IDEAS FOR . . . Checking Comprehension**
>
> Ask what students found most surprising about the information in the lecture. What other similarities were found between the Jim Twins? What does the case of the Jim Twins prove? Can they think of any explanations for these similarities? Why are some identical twins similar and some different?

After Listening

Survey

- Review the words in the box and ask students to give examples of behavior for each of these characteristics.

- You may want to assign a different word to each student.

- Model by asking several students questions using one of these words.

Exploring Spoken English

(pages 8–9)

45 mins

Language Function: Making Small Talk

- Ask students how they would start up a conversation with somebody. Ask: *What topics do you think are most common? What differences have you noticed between small talk in your home country and the U.S. or another country?*

- Read the information in the box and ask if students agree with it and if it is true in their countries.

track 1-06

Exercise A.

- Briefly discuss the photo. Ask: *Who are they? Where are they? What do you think they are saying?*

- Play the audio while students read.

- Ask some general questions about the setting and the speakers. For example, *Do the speakers know each other? Are they young or old? What can you tell about their personality or mood?*

- Ask specific questions about the conversations. For example: *What personal information does the first speaker give?*

Answer Key

Conversation 1
A: <u>Where are you from?</u>
B: I'm from Thailand. <u>Where are you from?</u>
A: I'm from Japan. <u>What do you do?</u>
B: I am a student. <u>What do you do?</u>
A: I am a writer.
B: It's nice to meet you.
A: Nice to meet you, too.

Conversation 2
A: <u>It's cold today, isn't it?</u>
B: Yes! The weather is different from yesterday!
A: Yes. <u>Yesterday was so hot!</u>
B: I know. And, today it is freezing! Very strange!
A: I agree.

Exercise B.

You may want to compare the two conversation topics and say how they are similar or different.

Answer Key

Answers should include where they are from, what they do, and the weather.

Exercise C.

- If you feel it is helpful, play the audio line by line so that students can repeat using the same intonation.

- Pair students to practice the conversations.

Grammar: The Simple Present and the Simple Past Tense of the Verb *Be*

- Introduce the information in the chart.

- Ask some questions. For example, *When do we use the form* am? *Or* is? *How many past forms of* be *are there? How is the negative formed?*

- You may want to ask students to test each other in pairs. For example, *Give an example of the present tense negative form with* he.

IDEAS FOR . . . Presenting Grammar

To practice the different forms of the verb *be*, you may want to use a simple substitution drill. Direct students to respond individually or as a class.

Example
Teacher: I am an athlete. *(pause)* She.
Student: She is an athlete.
Teacher: They.
Student: They are athletes.
Teacher: He.
Student: He is an athlete.

You can also practice contractions.
Teacher: I am an athlete.
Student: I'm an athlete.
Teacher: They are athletes.
Student: They're athletes.
Teacher: He is an athlete.
Student: He's an athlete.

---

track 1-07

Exercise A.

- Allow a few minutes for students to read the conversation and predict the answers.

- Play the audio while students write.

- Check the answers as a class.

- If necessary, play the audio again and point out intonation, stress, and use of contractions.

Answer Key

1. am 2. is 3. are 4. was 5. is 6. is 7. are 8. are 9. is
10. Were 11. was 12. were

Exercise B.

■ Pair students to create a new conversation.

■ Monitor their work and give feedback. Volunteers can present their conversation to the class.

 TIP Tell students to give each other feedback on grammar, pronunciation, and intonation.

Exploring Spoken English

(page 10)

Exercise C.

■ Find out if any students have a blog or use a social networking Web site. Ask: *What kind of pictures or information do you put on your page? Who reads your page?*

■ Tell students to look at the photos on Tony's page and describe them. Tell them to guess where the people are from, how old they are, what they do, and what their personalities are like.

■ Allow time for students to complete their answers and compare them with a partner. Check the answers by asking volunteers to read sentences aloud.

Answer Key

1. am 2. was 3. am not 4. am 5. is 6. is 7. is 8. is not
9. is 10. is 11. is 12. was 13. is 14. are 15. were 16. is
17. was 18. were 19. were

Exercise D. | Self-Reflection

■ You may want to start by brainstorming some personality adjectives and writing them on the board.

■ Discuss the meaning of the adjectives in the chart. For example, carefree (= someone without worries, opposite of nervous or worried), outgoing (= sociable, good at making friends), shy (= quiet, not confident, opposite of outgoing).

■ Allow time for students to reflect and complete their own charts.

■ Monitor students as they work, providing vocabulary help as needed.

Exercise E. | Follow-Up

■ Ask volunteers to present their descriptions.

■ Give feedback on correct use of the verb *be.*

 30-45 mins

Speaking *(page 11)*

Conducting a Survey

Exercise A.

■ Give students time to write their own answers.

■ You may want to practice the pronunciation, word stress, and intonation of each question before students work in pairs.

Exercise B. | Pair Work

■ Explain that the Venn diagram presents the information from exercise **A** in a different way. It makes it easy to see similarities and differences.

■ Explain that this type of diagram is a very useful academic skill for preparing presentations and essays or taking notes.

■ Monitor students as they work to make sure they understand the concept of the diagram.

Exercise C. | Presentation

■ Tell each pair of students to present their information to another pair of students.

■ Write some sentences on the board to help them get started. For example: *We have many differences but also several similarities. One difference is . . . . . Another difference is . . . .*

TIP It may be helpful to draw this diagram on the board. Ask two students to give you their information, and have other students tell you where to write each piece of information.

IDEAS FOR . . . Multi-level Classes

You can organize pairs of students in different ways. One option is to pair students according to their level, in same-level pairs. This will give you a chance to give extra help to those who are having difficulty.

Another option is to pair students with someone of a higher level so that they can get help from their partner.

---

30 mins

Viewing: Coming of Age
(pages 12–13)

Overview of the Video

The video describes a coming of age ritual for young Fulani boys in Mali. During the wet season, they have to lead the cows to drier lands to find food and bring them back safely. This signifies the boys' transition to adulthood.

WARM-UP

- Discuss the title of the video and ask if students know about any coming of age customs in other countries.
- Vocabulary note: the *Fulani* people are an ethnic group living in many African countries, mainly in West Africa.

Before Viewing

Exercise A. | Critical Thinking

- Go over the information in the chart, explaining any new words.
- Gather ideas from the class about possible reasons for these customs.

Vocabulary Note

Aborigine (= people originally from this region), wilderness (= natural and wild area where no one lives), ceremony (= formal ritual for special occasions like weddings and funerals).

Exercise B. | Predicting Content

- Emphasize that there are no right or wrong answers.
- Explain that students will add more ideas to the diagram after viewing the video.

Exercise C. | Using a Dictionary

Tell students to fill in the answers first before checking their dictionaries.

Answer Key

1. d **2.** a **3.** e **4.** b **5.** c

While Viewing

Exercise A.

- Play the video once for students to get the main idea.
- Give students time to add more ideas to the diagrams.

Exercise B.

- Allow time for students to read the statements before watching.
- Play the video while students complete the activity.

Answer Key

1. T **2.** F **3.** F **4.** T **5.** T

> **TIP** When playing the video for a second time, pause the video at any points that students found difficult in the first viewing.

> **IDEAS FOR ...** Checking Comprehension
>
> Play the video again and form groups to write questions about it. Afterwards, you may want to organize a competition where teams try to answer each others' questions.

After Viewing

Exercise A. | Critical Thinking

Call on students to read the information in the chart and discuss their opinions of these customs.

Answer Key

Answers will vary.

Exercise B. | Discussion

Ask volunteers to describe coming of age ceremonies in their culture to the class. Direct the other students to ask questions about these descriptions.

> **IDEAS FOR ...** Expansion
>
> Assign students to find out about coming of age customs in another country. They can present the information to the class in the next lesson.

Building Vocabulary
(page 14)

Exercise A.
track 1-08

- Model the pronunciation or play the audio for each word and tell students to repeat.

- Find out which words they know, but don't discuss the meanings yet, as this will come up in exercise **B**.

Exercise B. | Meaning from Context
track 1-09

- Play the audio while students read.

- Ask questions about any new vocabulary (not the target vocabulary); for example: *bank account, right-handed.*

- Ask students to try to define *typical.*

IDEAS FOR . . . **Checking Comprehension**

Check comprehension by asking questions about the information in the reading. Then have students create their own questions for the class.

For example:
How tall is a typical man in Holland?
How long does a typical woman in Japan live?

Ask students to suggest possible explanations for any of these statements.

Exercise C.

- Allow time for students to work individually.

- Then compare answers as a class.

Answer Key

1. female 2. billion 3. one of a kind 4. male 5. special
6. typical 7. Earth 8. alike

Using Vocabulary *(page 15)*

Exercise A.

- Do the first sentence as an example.

- Check the answers by asking volunteers to read the sentences aloud.

- Compare the meanings of typical (= usual), one of a kind (= unique), alike (= similar), and special (= different from others).

Answer Key

1. Earth 2. special 3. males 4. one of a kind 5. typical
6. alike 7. billion 8. females

Exercise B. | Discussion

- Form pairs to compare their answers to this question.

- Ask volunteers to report on the most surprising points of their discussion.

Exercise C. | Critical Thinking

- To introduce this exercise, you may want to say some sentences about the class that you know are unlikely to be true, and ask students to correct them. For example: *A typical person in this class comes to school by taxi.*

- Allow enough time for students to write as many sentences as they can.

- Then ask volunteers to read their sentences aloud.

- Ask the rest of the class whether or not they agree.

- You can also tell students to raise their hands in response to each sentence to show whether they think it is true.

- Give feedback on grammar as well as content.

- Look at the photo. As an extra activity, ask students to say sentences about a typical person in the city where this photo was taken.

Critical Thinking Focus

- Read the **Critical Thinking Focus** box. Ask students for some examples of how they might reflect before a class discussion. Give some examples of possible topics.

- Ask how this reflection task made them reflect critically and what they learned from it.

TIP When giving feedback, remember to praise students for taking risks and trying to use new vocabulary. Remind students that it is important to try out new language and not be afraid of making mistakes.

Developing Listening Skills

(pages 16–17)

45 mins

Before Listening

Exercise A. | Using a Dictionary

track 1-10

- Play the audio with students repeating.
- Find out which words students are familiar with and ask for example sentences, if possible.
- For unfamiliar words, tell students to use their dictionaries. You may want to point out that dictionaries often give more than one definition, and that the exact meaning of a word often depends on its context.

Exercise B.

- Allow time for students to work individually.
- Allow students to use their dictionaries, if necessary.

Answer Key

1. media 2. troublemaker 3. be in trouble 4. lazy
5. hang out with 6. impact

Exercise C. | Understanding Visuals

- Tell students to describe the two photos.
- Tell students to come up with as many different answers as possible.

Listening: A Conversation

Exercise A. | Critical Thinking

track 1-11

- Explain that you will play the audio once for students to get a general idea.
- Ask what the main problem with Carmen is. Discuss the problem as a class and evaluate Kathryn's response to the situation.

Exercise B. | Listening for Details

track 1-11

- Read the example and emphasize the use of past tense and the position in the chart.
- Monitor students as they write to check on any problems.
- Draw the chart on the board and choose individual students to come to the board and write their answers.
- Check the answers as a class.

Answer Key

Carmen Before	Carmen Now
good student	lazy
good listener	troublemaker
good girl	hard time
hard worker	bad student
great sister	not happy

After Listening

Exercise A. | Follow-Up

Answer Key

Answers will vary. Possible answers include:

Carmen was a good student.
Carmen was a good listener.
Carmen was a good girl.
Carmen was a hard worker.
Carmen was a great sister.
Carmen is lazy.
Carmen is a troublemaker.
Carmen is a bad student.
Carmen is not happy.

Exercise B. | Discussion

- Form groups. Tell students to discuss their answers.
- Remind students to practice using the new words from this lesson.
- Ask a volunteer from each group to summarize some of the most interesting answers from their group.

IDEAS FOR . . . Expansion

Ask students to think of a similar situation that has affected them, a family member, or a friend. Ask them to explain the situation to their group. Two members in the group will role-play a conversation about the problem situation (similar to the conversation they listened to in this lesson). Afterwards, the original student can give feedback on how accurate the conversation was. Ask volunteers to present their conversations to the class, and ask them for ideas for possible solutions to the problem situation.

30 mins

Exploring Spoken English
(pages 18–19)

Grammar: *Wh-* Questions with the Verb *Be*

- Explain that these five question words are known as *Wh-* question words (even though one begins with *H*).
- Ask what kind of information each word asks about (who = people, what = things, where = places, why = reasons, how = the way something feels, looks, or is done).
- Practice the pronunciation of each word if necessary. (Point out that /w/ in *who* is silent and the word begins with the sound /h/.)
- Ask students to describe the word order in these questions. What word follows the question word? (the verb *be*). What word follows the verb? (the subject).

Exercise A.

Allow time for students to complete their answers individually.

Answer Key

1. Who are they?
2. Where are you from?
3. Why was she nervous?
4. What country are you from?
5. How were the twins different?
6. Who is his twin brother?

Exercise B.

- Students may work individually or in pairs.
- Tell students to come up with as many questions as possible, and to share them with the class.

Answer Key

Answers will vary.

Exercise C.

- Higher-level students may be able to complete the questions without looking at the box.
- Ask students to suggest who might be speaking in this conversation (mother and daughter? roommates? sisters?).
- Allow time for students to write their answers.

- Choose students to read out different lines of the conversation.
- Give feedback on pronunciation, stress, and intonation.

TIP To provide extra practice with intonation, you may want to suggest that each partner takes a specific role (for example, parent; best friend) or a specific mood (for example, angry; worried).

Answer Key

A: Hi. <u>Where were you last night?</u>
B: I was at the movies.
A: <u>Who was there?</u>
B: Sam and I were there together.
A: <u>How is he?</u>
B: He is good.
A: <u>What was the movie about?</u>
B: It was about a teenager. He was sad, but he changed. In the end, he was happy.
A: <u>Who is the actor?</u>
B: I don't remember his name. I'm tired. I'm going to bed.
A: <u>Why are you tired?</u>
B: It is late! Good night!

Exercise D.

- Pair students to practice the conversations.
- Walk around the room to monitor their pronunciation and intonation (see Tip above).
- Choose pairs to present their conversation to the class.
- Ask other students in the class to give feedback that is constructive and helpful.

Exercise E.

- You may want to form groups with all students from the same country, or groups with students from different countries.
- Encourage students to disagree and argue their point of view by giving reasons and examples (perhaps from their own experience).
- You may want to start by giving some of your own examples for the first sentence.
- Point out the **Student to Student** box. Explain the importance of interrupting politely.

Answer Key

Answers will vary.

Engage: Giving a Presentation about Yourself

45 mins

(page 20)

WARM-UP

- Discuss different types of visuals that can be used in presentations: graphs, charts, diagrams, photos, illustrations, cartoons.

- Discuss why it is important to have clear visuals to accompany a presentation.

- Discuss the features of good visuals (clear, easy to read, not too complicated, good use of color). You may want to refer back to other visuals in this unit, such as the map on pages 2–3 and the Venn diagram on page 11.

- Read out the task. Explain that this presentation will be very short and easy and will introduce skills they will need in academic presentations later on.

Exercise A. | Self-Reflection

- Tell students to read the sample pie chart and explain the meaning of the different sections.

- Brainstorm ideas for other things that might impact you. For example: job, religion, art/music.

- Allow time for students to complete their charts individually.

- Ask students to think carefully about how each of these aspects impacts their lives and to think of at least one example of each. They can take notes.

Exercise B. | Planning a Presentation

- Read the presentation aloud, pausing frequently, making eye contact with the class, and holding up the book to point the pie chart.

- You may want to ask students to practice this presentation in pairs or small groups to get a feel for the skills such as making eye contact and pausing. (Sometimes it is easier to practice with information that is not personal.)

- Point out the order in which the information is presented (from most to least impact).

- Allow time for students to plan their own presentations.

Presentation Skills: Making Eye Contact

- Read the information in the box.

- Demonstrate giving the presentation in exercise **B** without making eye contact, by looking down at the ground, for example, or looking at the book or your notes all the time. Explain that this makes the presentation less interesting and does not engage the audience.

Exercise C. | Practice Your Presentation

- Students may practice in pairs or small groups.

- Direct other students to give feedback on presentation skills: speaking clearly, pausing, making eye contact, and pointing to the visual.

- Put students into groups and ask them to choose their roles.

> **TIP** Giving a presentation can be very intimidating for students who have never done this before. As this is the first one, you may want to ask each group to present to another group, rather than to the whole class.

Exercise D. | Presentation

- Ask volunteers to give their presentation to the class.

- As this is the first presentation, it may be best to focus only on positive feedback. Which students had presentations that were well organized? Who did well at making eye contact, speaking clearly, pausing often, and pointing to the visual?

> **TIP** You may want to video or audio record the presentations. Later, students can watch or listen to the recordings to evaluate their progress.

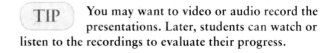

Taking Risks

Academic Pathways

Lesson A: Listening to a Radio Show
                                      Discussing a Plan

Lesson B: Listening to a Conversation
                                      Giving a Group Presentation

Unit Theme

Unit 2 explores the topic of being adventurous and taking risks. The unit includes photographs and descriptions of a number of extreme sports, which are becoming increasingly popular.

Think and Discuss *(page 21)*

5 mins

- Ask students to describe the photo.

- Ask: *Is this diver taking a risk? What possible dangers does the diver face?*

- Brainstorm ideas about what the diver is doing. For example, taking pictures, making a film, collecting research data.

- Find out what students know about sharks.

Note: There are about 400 species of sharks. They feed on plankton, squid, and small fish. They mostly live in oceans and seas, although some live in rivers. Sharks have up to 5 sets of replaceable teeth. When one tooth is damaged, it is replaced by another. They can have up to 3,000 teeth at a time. Some well-known larger species are the great white shark, the blue shark, and the hammerhead shark.

Exploring the Theme

15 mins

(pages 22–23)

The opening spread features people engaged in a number of different types of extreme sports.

- Ask students to describe each activity and say if they have had any experience of it (skateboarding, snowboarding, kickboxing or martial arts, rock climbing).

- Practice reading the numbers (for example: eight point four million people).

- Point out that these numbers in the millions refer to the number of people in the U.S. who do these activities. Ask students to think about the number of people who do these activities in their countries. Ask: *Are these sports popular in your country? Why or why not? Do you think the number of people his higher or lower in your country? Why?*

- Discuss why people are attracted to these different sports. Which one would your students like to try? Why or why not?

- Discuss the possible dangers of these sports.

- Read the questions and discuss the answers as a class.

IDEAS FOR . . . Expansion

Students can brainstorm a list of other types of extreme sports. Write them on the board.

Have students choose one extreme sport and find out some information about it for homework. Students can bring in a picture and tell the class about their sport in the next lesson.

Possible examples: hang gliding, ski jumping, sky diving, caving, motocross, cliff diving, whitewater kayaking, kite surfing, bungee jumping.

Building Vocabulary

30 mins

(page 24)

WARM-UP

The Lesson A target vocabulary is presented in the context of different kinds of adventure activities.

Ask students to describe:

- what kind of trips and vacations they enjoy or think they would enjoy.
- the most exciting trip they have ever had.

track 1-12

Exercise A.

- Tell students to read the words aloud, and check the ones they already know.
- Correct pronunciation or stress if necessary.
- If appropriate, pair students to explain the words they know to a partner.
- Play the audio and have students repeat each word (optional).

track 1-13

Exercise B. | Meaning from Context

- Draw students' attention to the photograph. Ask: *What kind of adjectives describe this place?* (for example: *peaceful, beautiful, cold, calm, cruel, silent*)
- Discuss the meaning of the word *glacier* (= a river of ice that moves very slowly) and optionally *iceberg* (= large piece of ice floating in the sea). Find out if students have ever visited a place like this (a glacier, or mountains).
- Tell students to read the article, paying special attention to the words in blue.
- Play the audio if you think it is helpful.
- Ask questions to check the meaning of any of the words that are not in blue (for example: *parachute, cliff-jump, dive, hike, raft*).
- Ask if any students have ever tried any of these activities.

Exercise C. | Using a Dictionary

- Allow time for students to complete their answers individually.
- As you check the answers, ask students what part of speech each word is.
- Model the correct pronunciation of any difficult words, or play the audio from exercise **A**.
- Point out two ways to form adjectives from nouns. For example: *risk (risky), danger (dangerous)*.

Answer Key

1. c 2. d 3. f 4. g 5. h 6. b 7. a 8. e

IDEAS FOR . . . Checking Comprehension

Ask additional questions about the text or write them on the board. (Possible answers are in parentheses.)

1. Why do people like adventure trips? (to do something different, to get a thrill)
2. What do all these activities have in common? (they are risky, dangerous, exciting)
3. What do you imagine that trips to the Sahara Desert and the Grand Canyon are like? (The Sahara would be very hot and dry, might involve traveling by camel or by jeep. The Grand Canyon could involve hiking, climbing, and camping, as well as cycling, and also might be hot and dry in summer.)
4. Do you think that a trip by boat to the glacier would be dangerous? Why? (freezing conditions, you might get hit by falling ice)

Using Vocabulary *(page 25)*

30 mins

Exercise A.

- Do the first item as an example. (Have a volunteer explain or mime the word *bite* if necessary.)
- Allow time for students to complete the exercise individually.
- Pair students to take turns reading out the sentences to each other.
- Monitor students as they practice and give tips on pronunciation.
- Have volunteers read out the sentences to the class.

Answer Key

1. risky 2. seeks 3. popular 4. exciting 5. extreme
6. adventure 7. thrill 8. danger

> **TIP** As an extension, students can make up their own sentences using as many of these words as they can. You could make it a competition to see who can include the most words in one sentence.

Exercise B. | Discussion

- Ask students to describe the photo. Ask if this sport is popular in their country. Pair students to discuss the questions.
- Remind students to use the target words in their answers.
- Tell pairs of students to summarize their answers for each question and present them to the class.

45 mins

Developing Listening Skills
(pages 26–27)

Before Listening

Exercise A. | Using a Dictionary

- Practice the pronunciation of these words.

- Pair students with different dictionaries, if possible, to compare the definitions of these words. Tell them to be alert to differences in the definitions.

- Point out that the prefix *in-* makes a word into its opposite. Other examples: *indefinite, incorrect, inappropriate.* Gather additional examples for students.

- Mention that the word *set* has a variety of meanings and is used in many idiomatic expressions and phrasal verbs for example: *set up, set out, set off.*

Exercise B.

- Give students time to complete the exercise individually.

- Ask students to make predictions about the radio show based on the vocabulary.

Answer Key

1. incredible 2. set a record 3. adventurer 4. avalanche

Exercise C. | Predicting Content

- Ask students to describe the photos and make sentences using the vocabulary below them.

- Emphasize that there is no right or wrong answer at this stage.

- Remind students why it is important to predict content before listening. (In order to prepare your mind to receive new information and assimilate it more easily.)

Answer Key

Answers will vary.

Listening: A Radio Show

track 1-14

Exercise A. | Listening for Main Ideas

- Play the audio.

- Tell students to read and circle their answers.

- Compare answers as a class.

Answer Key

The following main ideas should be circled:

Adventurers take risks because they seek adventure. Adventures can have dangers.

track 1-14

Exercise B. | Listening for Details

- Have students read the questions and answer choices.

- Play the audio again while students complete the exercise.

- Have students compare answers in pairs.

- Play the audio or sections of it again if necessary.

Answer Key

1. b 2. a 3. b 4. c 5. a

IDEAS FOR . . .   Checking Comprehension

Ask students why these three adventurers were on the show. (Answer: They were finalists in the *National Geographic* Adventurers of the Year contest.)

Ask students what geographical places are mentioned in the audio. You may need to play the audio again and ask students to raise their hands when they hear the name of a geographical place.

(Answers: Gasherbrum II, Pakistan, Mount Everest, Indian/Nepali border, the Ganges River, the Indian Ocean)

After Listening

Discussion

- Review the words in the box.

- Explain that students should check one box for each adjective.

- You may want to give an example first to get students started: *I think . . . . . . is more dangerous because . . . . . .*

- Have each pair present one opinion to the class, and find out if their classmates agree.

45 mins

Exploring Spoken English
(pages 28–29)

Grammar: The Simple Present Tense

- Tell students to read the examples in the chart. Then ask some questions.

- When do we use the simple present? (for repeated actions and habits)

- Look at the affirmative statements. When do we use *s* with the verb? (with *he, she,* or *it*)

- Look at the negative statements. How do we form negative statements? (by adding *do + not* or *does + not* before the verb)

- When do we use *does* with the verb? (with *he, she,* or *it*)

- Point out that there is no *s* after a verb with *doesn't*.

- What is the word order in *yes/no* questions?

IDEAS FOR . . . Presenting Grammar

Brainstorm a list of activities that students do regularly. Include sports and free time activities. Make a list on the board.

Tell students to raise their hands if they regularly do the first activity. Then select a student to say a sentence about him or herself (I swim or I don't swim), about another student (Peter swims / Leo doesn't swim), and about two other students (Marie and Alicia swim / they don't swim). Repeat this process with another activity and different students.

Exercise A.

- Ask students to look at the pictures.

- Point out that the first picture has an X and therefore the statement is negative.

- Allow time for students to write sentences.

- Choose volunteers to come to the board and write their answers.

Answer Key

Sentences may be in a different order. **1.** He surfs. **2.** He doesn't swim. **3.** He plays tennis. **4.** He rock climbs. **5.** He doesn't hike.

Exercise B. | Discussion

- Have students work in pairs to discuss which of these activities are dangerous and why Mike prefers some activities and not others.

- Encourage students to use the simple present tense. For example: *He skis because it is exciting. He rock climbs because it is dangerous.*

Exercise C.

- Pair students to complete the chart.

- Model one or two exchanges with a student.

Answer Key

Answers will vary.

Exercise D. | Follow-Up

- Nominate students to tell the class about their partner.

- Remind students to make both affirmative and negative statements.

- Focus on correcting errors with the third person singular.

- After a student has finished, ask other students to see if they can remember all the information.

- As an additional activity, ask students to make questions and statements about the diver in the picture. For example: *He swims under the ice. He uses an oxygen cylinder. He wears a diving suit.*

TIP As errors can frequently occur with the third person singular, it is a good idea to develop a sign or signal to point out the missing *s*. You can write a large *s* on a wall poster and point to it, or you can prepare a flashcard with the symbol *s* and raise it at the appropriate time.

Exploring Spoken English
(page 30)

Pronunciation: The Third Person Singular
track 1-15

- Explain that the pronunciation (and spelling) of the third person singular /s/ ending depends on the previous consonant or vowel. Give some examples.
- Write the three different sounds on the board.
- Give each sound a number 1, 2, or 3.
- Say some example words and ask students to identify which end sound they have by saying the correct number (e.g., *sound number 1*, etc.).
- Present the information in the box and play the audio.
- Ask some questions. For example: Which sound comes after the sound /ch/ as in *watch*? (answer: /iz/ watches).

Exercise A.
track 1-16

- Tell students to read the verbs and try to predict which sound each one has before listening.
- Play the audio while students write their answers.
- Play the audio again, pausing after each one. Check the answers with students repeating (individually or as a class).

Answer Key

Words with /s/ sound: kayaks, hikes, surfs, bikes, bungee jumps.

Words with /z/ sound: climbs, skis, snowboards, swims.

Words with /iz/ sound: watches.

Exercise B.
track 1-17

- Check the answers by asking students to say sentences, such as, *She surfs. She doesn't bike.*
- Correct the pronunciation of final sound /s/ individually and as a group.
- Model asking and answering question about the first picture with a student. For example: *Does Maria surf? B: Yes, she surfs.*

Answer Key

The following activities should be checked: surf, cliff jump, ski, kayak, rock climb, and snowboard.

Speaking *(page 31)*

30-45 mins

Discussing a Plan

Exercise A. | Survey

- Explain that the survey will help them find out how adventurous they are.
- Give students time to read the questions and ask you about any difficult vocabulary.
- Poll the class for each question and ask volunteers to explain reasons for their choices.

Answer Key

Answers will vary.

IDEAS FOR . . . Expansion

Ask student to add one or two questions to the survey. Ask them to pose their questions to the class.

Lead a class discussion about when it is a good idea to be brave and take risks, and when it might be foolish.

Discuss different types of bravery or courage. For example, taking physical risks to do a sport, or to help other people.

Exercise B. | Critical Thinking

- Discuss the categories shown and give some examples of your own. For the category Activity, you may refer students to the picture and say *I want to try hang-gliding.*
- Read the example plan and explain that students will choose a category and write three *different* ways of achieving their goal.
- Monitor students as they work to make sure they understand the concept of the plan.

Answer Key

Answers will vary.

Exercise C. | Comparing

Have students stand up and sit with someone who chose the same category.

Exercise D.

- Have pairs stand up again and join a pair who chose a different category, if possible.
- If any students finish early, ask them to choose another category and make another plan.

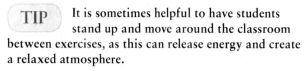

TIP It is sometimes helpful to have students stand up and move around the classroom between exercises, as this can release energy and create a relaxed atmosphere.

Viewing: Highlining Yosemite Falls *(pages 32–33)*

30 mins

Overview of the Video

The video presents the experience of a man who enjoys highlining in Yosemite Valley.

WARM-UP

Use a map to show students the location of Yosemite National Park. Explain what national parks are and what activities people do there (for example: camping, hiking, climbing). Ask if any students have been to Yosemite or to any other national park.

Before Viewing

Exercise A. | Prior Knowledge

- Ask students to describe the activity of highlining.
- Draw the chart on the board and complete the first column with ideas from the class.

Answer Key

Answers will vary.

TIP You can use the chart from exercise A later in the lesson to check whether students' questions were answered in the video. If not, assign these questions as research for homework.

Exercise B. | Using a Dictionary

Check the pronunciation of these words if necessary.

Answer Key

1. e 2. a 3. d 4. b 5. c

Exercise C. | Predicting Content

Emphasize that there are no correct answers at this stage. (They will check their predictions when watching the video.)

Answer Key

1. distractions 2. focuses 3. lunatic 4. beauty
5. creativity

Exercise D.

- Ask for an example question for the second column.
- Refer to the chart on the board and complete the second column using ideas from the class.

While Viewing

Exercise A. | Checking Predictions

Give time for students to compare answers.

Exercise B.

- Give time for students to read through the statements before watching again.
- Check the answers and ask students to correct any false sentences.

Answer Key

1. T 2. T 3. F 4. F

Exercise C. | Using the Simple Present

- Give time for students to read through the answer choices before watching again.
- Ask which *s* sound each verb has.

Answer Key

The following things should be circled: use Amsteel, focus on his breath, set up his cable, walk the line, focus on the beauty, use a safety belt

The following things should be crossed out: focus on the moving water, sleep on the line

Exercise D.

Tell students to complete the column with their own ideas and compare with a partner.

After Viewing

Exercise A. | Discussion

Ask students to give examples from their own experience to support their opinions.

Exercise B. | Self-Reflection

Write the following sentence on the board for students to try to complete in as many ways as they can.

I see a new part of myself when I . . .

Building Vocabulary

(page 34)

30 mins

track 1-18

Exercise A.

- Model the pronunciation or play the audio of each word and ask students to repeat.
- Ask which words they know, but don't discuss the meanings yet, as this will come up in exercise **B**.

track 1-19

Exercise B. | Meaning from Context

- Ask students to describe the photo. Ask: *What is this person doing and why?*
- Play the audio as students read the article (optional).
- Answer questions about any new vocabulary (not the target vocabulary).
- Remind students of the meaning of *set a record* from Lesson **A** (= to be the best at something).

Vocabulary Note

rain forest (n) forests in the tropical zone near the equator where there is high rainfall, such as the Amazon Rainforest.

Exercise C.

- Allow time for students to work individually.
- Ask students to tell you the answers as you write them on the board.

Answer Key

1. explorer 2. explore 3. satisfy 4. needs 5. act
6. discoveries 7. make a fortune 8. information

IDEAS FOR ... Checking Comprehension

Ask these additional questions about the information in the reading or write them on the board and have students discuss them in pairs.

1. How many people are mentioned in the reading? (two)
2. How are they different? (one explores forests, the other explores oceans)
3. How are they similar? (they are both explorers and have risky but important jobs)
4. What kind of information could these explorers learn? (answers will vary, but possibly something that will help medical science, biology, or the environment)

Using Vocabulary

(page 35)

Exercise A.

- Do the first sentence as an example.
- Check the answers by asking volunteers to read the sentences aloud.

Answer Key

1. explore 2. make a fortune 3. act 4. discoveries
5. needs 6. information 7. satisfy 8. Explorers

Exercise B. | Discussion

- Have students work in pairs to compare their answers to this question.
- Ask volunteers to report on the most surprising points of their discussion.
- Compile a list on the board of examples of *daily needs, discoveries,* and *ways of making a fortune.*

Exercise C. | Ranking Information

- Explain that students will write a number next to each reason according to how important they think it is.
- Have students write their numbers individually first. Then compare their answers in pairs.
- Compare answers as a class, by compiling a number of votes for the best reason.
- Ask students if they can suggest any additional reasons to explore.
- Ask students for examples of famous explorers and what they think their reasons were.

Answer Key

Answers will vary.

Developing Listening Skills

45 mins

(pages 36–37)

Before Listening

Exercise A. | Using a Dictionary

- Play the audio and ask students to repeat each word (optional).
- Point out word families. For example, *adventurous (adj), adventure (n); sickness (n), sick (adj); unexplored (adj), explore (v), explorer (n).*
- Ask for examples of other words ending in *-ous (dangerous, famous)* and *-ness (illness, kindness).*

Exercise B.

- Allow time for students to work individually.
- Check the answers and write them on the board.
- Point out other meanings of the word *rough* (violent, not smooth) and other collocations such as *a rough storm, a rough neighborhood, a rough road.*

Answer Key

1. unexplored **2.** rough **3.** flooded **4.** protect
5. sickness **6.** adventurous

Critical Thinking Focus

Discuss the importance of predicting and ask for some examples of how prediction could be useful before listening to academic lectures and seminars.

Exercise C. | Predicting Content

- Emphasize that it is not important to get the correct answers here, but only to start thinking about the topic.
- Tell students to look at the photo and describe the woman: her appearance, her personality, her environment.

Listening: A Conversation

track 1-20

Exercise A. | Listening for the Main Idea

- Play the audio. Then compare answers as a class.
- If there is disagreement, play the audio again before checking the answers.

Answer Key

The following main idea should be circled: **3.** The work of Emma Stokes.

track 1-20

Exercise B. | Listening for Details

- Allow time for students to read the sentences.
- Play the audio.
- Have students compare answers in pairs.
- Then check answers as a class.

Answer Key

The following details should be circled:

She camped on an elephant nest.
She discovered 125,000 gorillas.
The area was flooded.
They slept in beds hung from trees.
Companies and sickness are dangerous to the gorillas.

track 1-20

Exercise C. | Checking Predictions

- Ask students to look back at their predictions and tell the class which ones they guessed correctly.
- Play the audio again if necessary.

After Listening

Critical Thinking

- Have students look at the photo and read the examples.
- Assign students to groups to compare their answers.
- Remind students to use the new words from this lesson.
- Nominate a volunteer from each group to summarize some of the most interesting answers from their group.

Answer Key

Answers will vary.

IDEAS FOR . . . Expansion

Ask students to role-play an interview with an explorer on a radio show using the information they have written.

Ask students to think of a famous explorer and to imagine they are explaining the reasons for their trip. The partner will try to guess who they are.

Examples: Marco Polo, Christopher Columbus, Amelia Earhart, Roald Amundsen, Edmund Hillary, Neil Armstrong.

Exploring Spoken English
(pages 38–39)

Grammar: The Simple Present with *Wh-* Questions

- Ask students to name the five *wh-* question words.
- Ask what kind of information each one asks for.
- Practice pronunciation if necessary.
- Ask students to study the chart and tell you about the word order in these questions.

  What word follows the question word? (the verb *do*)
  What word follows the verb? (the subject)
  What word follows the subject? (the main verb)
  Does the main verb change? (no)
  Which verb changes in the third person? (*do* changes to *does*)

- Ask students to make example questions using the words in the chart.
- Read the sample questions and responses. Ask students to rewrite them using a different subject.

> **IDEAS FOR . . . Presenting Grammar**
>
> Write the answers to five different questions on the board and have students figure out what the questions are.
>
> Examples:
> I go surfing. (What do you do on the weekends?)

- Allow time for students to complete their answers individually.
- Ask volunteers to come to the board and write their answers.
- Invite students to ask *wh-* questions about the photo. Make a list on the board.

Answer Key

1. When do you hike?
2. Where does he swim?
3. How do they rock climb?
4. What activity do you do?
5. Why does she paraglide?
6. What do they do on the weekend?
7. Why does she take risks?
8. Where does he bike?

Language Function: Showing Interest

- Role-play two conversations with a student, one where you show interest using these expressions and one where you show no interest at all.
- Ask how the other person feels if you show no interest.
- Practice saying these expressions using appropriate intonation.
- Ask if they can add any other expressions. (For example: *Mmhmm. Oh yes? Is that right? Amazing!*)

Exercise A.

Ask students to check their answers, or add other activities to the list if they wish.

Answer Key

Answers will vary.

Exercise B.

- Ask students to look at the photo and suggest *wh-* questions to ask this person.
- Write the questions on the board and ask students to correct any errors.
- Pair students to ask each other questions; they can refer to the questions on the board to help them.
- Ask for volunteers to present their conversation to the class.

Student to Student: Making Eye Contact

- Remind students about making eye contact when giving a presentation. Explain that it is important in conversations, too.
- You may want to mention that although staring continuously is not polite, looking down or away throughout the conversation is not polite either.

> **IDEAS FOR . . . Expansion**
>
> Invite a guest to visit the class and have your class prepare *wh-* questions to ask him or her. Review the questions before the visit.
>
> On the day of the visit, have students take notes of the answers so that you can discuss them as a class later.

Engage: Giving a Group Presentation *(page 40)*

45 mins

WARM-UP

- Bring in photos of different types of adventure activities.
- You can spread them out on a table and gather students around to discuss them and say which ones they like and why.

Exercise A. | Choose

- Go over the words in the box and make sure students understand them. You may want to call on individual students to explain each one.
- Have students form groups and discuss their chosen activity.

> **TIP** To form groups, you can ask students to walk around and get into groups according to the activity they have chosen.
>
> Alternatively, you can write the activities on paper signs and stick them around the classroom. Then ask students to stand under the sign for the activity they have chosen.

Exercise B. | Planning Your Trip

- Explain that in a group presentation, each member of the group will present one part of the presentation. They can help each other prepare what they are going to say. They should each speak for roughly equal amounts of time.
- Read the examples in the chart.
- Have students draw a chart and make notes in their notebooks.

Exercise C. | Planning a Presentation

- Have students practice in groups. Explain that they can use their notes, but will not read the text. They should say four or five sentences each.

- Give an example of how to expand on ideas in the notes. For example: *We can scuba dive. It's an exciting sport. You can go to interesting places and learn a lot about oceans and fish.*

Exercise D. | Presentation

- Invite groups to come to the front of the class and give their presentations.
- Encourage the rest of the class to ask *wh-* questions after each presentation.
- Remind students to give positive feedback and encouragement.
- Give positive feedback on content and organization of ideas, speaking clearly, eye contact, and asking for questions.

Presentation Skills: Asking for Questions

- Read the information in the box.
- Practice the pronunciation and intonation of these questions.
- Suggest that they nominate one person in each group to ask for questions at the end.

> **TIP** To help students develop confidence before giving their presentations, you may ask them to present to another group first. They can switch groups and do this several times so that they can get more practice.

> **IDEAS FOR . . . Expansion**
>
> You may want to have students give another presentation about a real trip that they are planning. Have other students in the class ask a lot of *wh-* questions to find out as many details as possible about the trip.

Enjoy the Ride!

Academic Pathways

Lesson A: Listening to an Interview
              Choosing the Best Idea

Lesson B: Listening to a Conversation
              Giving a Group Presentation

Unit Theme

Unit 3 explores the topic of transportation in different countries and developments in modern transportation methods.

Think and Discuss *(page 41)*

5 mins

- Write the word *transportation* in the center of the board and brainstorm types of transportation. (For example: train, bus, bicycle, motorbike, plane, car, ship, boat)
- Alternatively, give students two minutes to write as many types of transportation as possible. Then gather ideas on the board.
- Ask students to describe the photo. What is special or unusual about it?
- Discuss the questions and lead into general discussion about types of transportation and which ones are healthier, faster, safer, cheaper, or cleaner.

Exploring the Theme

15 mins

(pages 42–43)

The opening spread features people using different types of transportation and a bar chart showing how many people use public transportation in different countries.

- Discuss question 1. Ask students to describe each photo. Which type of transportation would they like/ not like to try? Why?
- Discuss question 2. Ask students to describe transportation in their town or city. Ask: *Is it private or public? Is it expensive? Do many people use it? Do you use it? Why or why not?*

- Ask students to explain what the bar chart shows. What do the different colors mean? When looking at the list of countries, ask which countries they predict use public transportation the most and the least. Does the bar chart support their predictions or not?
- Discuss some possible reasons for these different statistics. The reasons may differ for different countries.
- Prompt students to draw other conclusions from the information in the chart.

Vocabulary Note

Public transportation: any form of transportation with set fares and routes that is available to the public, such as train, bus, subway, ferry. It can be publicly or privately owned.

IDEAS FOR . . .   Expansion

Have students work in groups to create a survey of five questions about transportation use among their classmates.

Then select one member of each group to go to each of the other groups to collect the results. When they return to the original group, they can work together to compile a chart with all the data they have gathered in response to their questions.

Building Vocabulary *(page 44)*

30 mins

WARM-UP

The Lesson A target vocabulary is presented in the context of different ways to travel.

- Ask students to talk about what kind of travel methods they prefer and why.
- Ask for volunteers to describe the most unusual travel method they have ever tried.

 ### Exercise A. | Using a Dictionary

track 1-21

- Play the audio and pause for students to repeat each word.
- Ask volunteers to create and say some example sentences using these words in order to check comprehension.

 ### Exercise B. | Meaning from Context

track 1-22

- Tell students they will hear about three ways that people commute.
- Remind students to pay special attention to the words in blue.
- Give students time to complete the activity individually.
- Explain that one way of figuring out meaning is to look at words in the surrounding sentences. Look at the use of the word *vehicle* in the passage and explain how it is possible to figure out the meaning by looking at the previous sentence. (*A bus, a car, and a train are usual ways to move from one place to another. There are many other vehicles, too.*)

Answer Key

1. vehicle 2. safe 3. pedestrian 4. passenger
5. commute 6. share 7. convenient 8. crowded

IDEAS FOR . . . Checking Comprehension

Ask additional questions about the text or write them on the board.

1. Which types of transportation are for one person and which are for many people?
2. What kind of power does each one use?
3. What is safe or dangerous about each of these travel methods?

 # Using Vocabulary *(page 45)*

30 mins

Exercise A.

- Ask students to look at the photo and describe what kind of train this is and what it might be like to travel in it.
- Do the first item as an example.
- Allow time for students to complete their answers individually.

Answer Key

1. commute 2. crowded 3. convenient 4. vehicle
5. safe 6. pedestrians 7. share 8. passenger

Exercise B.

- Pair students to compare answers, and then read the conversation. Assign one partner A and the other B. Finally, tell them to switch roles.
- Monitor students as they practice and give tips on pronunciation. Focus on correct pronunciation of the new words and natural intonation and expression.
- Ask volunteers to present the conversation to the class.

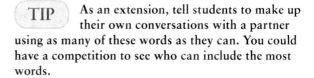 TIP   As an extension, tell students to make up their own conversations with a partner using as many of these words as they can. You could have a competition to see who can include the most words.

Exercise C. | Discussion

- Model answering these questions with your own responses.
- Remind students to use the target words in their discussion.

Exercise D. | Ranking Information

- Give an example. For example: *I think a bus is safer than a car because it doesn't go so fast.*
- You may want to do a quick review of comparative forms with adjectives.
- Ask group to share their ranking and defend their choices.

Answer Key

Answers will vary.

Developing Listening Skills

45 mins

(pages 46–47)

track 1-23

Pronunciation: *There is* and *There are*

- Contrast the pronunciation of *There is* and *There's*. Say each pair a few times and ask students to identify whether it is "careful" or "fast."

- Play the examples on the audio. Tell students to repeat either individually or as a group.

- Assign students to work in pairs to practice the sentences.

- Monitor students and choose one or two of the students with good pronunciation to say the sentences for the class.

track 1-24

Before Listening

Critical Thinking: Focus Listening for Order

- Explain that "key" words or "signpost" words can help you to improve your listening skills.

- Ask for some examples of situations when someone might give you directions or instructions. (For example: explaining a recipe, or how to use a gadget or machine, or how to get to someone's house.)

- Tell students to read the paragraph and try to predict the missing words. (More than one option may be possible.)

- Play the audio while students write the answers.

- Write the answers on the board and discuss which other words are also possible.

- Ask some comprehensions questions about the passage. For example: *Where are they going? How many modes of transport are mentioned? How long will the journey take?*

Answer Key

1. First 2. Second 3. Then 4. Finally

Listening: An Interview

track 1-25

Exercise A. | Listening for Main Ideas

- Tell students to read the questions.

- Play the audio while students circle their answers.

- Compare answers as a class.

Answer Key

1. b 2. c

track 1-25

Exercise B. | Listening for Details

- Have students read the statements, then play the audio.

- Refer to the photo to explain the meaning of *dog sled*.

- Ask students' opinions about the interview. What did they find interesting or surprising?

Answer Key

1. T 2. F 3. T 4. F 5. F

> **IDEAS FOR . . . Checking Comprehension**
>
> Ask these additional questions or write them on the board.
>
> 1. Why does Maria prefer traveling by tuk-tuk to traveling by bus? (They are safer.)
> 2. Why does Maria like traveling on top of the bus in Nepal? (It is not as crowded, and there is more fresh air.)

After Listening

Exercise A. | Critical Thinking

- Model this activity by describing how to get to your home from the school. Use key words for showing order in your description.

- Brainstorm a few different places in your students' countries. Write them on the board. They could be famous sights, cities, or places of natural beauty.

Answer Key

Answers will vary.

Exercise B. | Explaining

- Monitor students as they work in pairs.

- Provide feedback on use of key words and pronunciation.

- Have students change pairs two or more times.

Exploring Spoken English
(pages 48–49)

45 mins

Grammar: *There is, There are, There was, There were*

- Write two example sentences using *there is* and *there are* on the board, and ask students to explain the difference. (For example, *There is a map on the wall. There are twenty students in this class.*)

- Write two example sentences using *there was* and *there were* on the board and ask students to explain the difference. (For example, *There was a movie on TV last night. There were a lot of people on the bus this morning.*)

- Ask students to read aloud the examples in the chart, paying attention to pronunciation.

- Point out that the past tense example sentences include a time phrase that refers to the past.

IDEAS FOR ... Presenting Grammar

- Draw a diagram on the board to show singular, plural, past, and present.
- Point to the relevant part of the chart as you say each sentence from the chart in the student book.
- Ask a student to come to the board and point as you say each sentence.
- Call on students to say a sentence while another student points to the chart.

	past	present
singular		
plural		

Exercise A.

- Go over the first example with the class.
- Allow time for students to write their answers.
- Call on volunteers to read out their answers.

Answer Key

1. There are 2. There is 3. There were 4. There was
5. There are / There were 6. There is

Exercise B.

- Give one or two examples of past and present statements about your town.
- Monitor students' work as they discuss their answers in pairs.
- Call on volunteers to come to the board to write their sentences.
- Ask the others in the class to make any corrections.

Answer Key

Answers will vary.

Exercise C.

- Have students name things and people in the photo. (elephants, bicycles, mopeds, pedestrians, boys, men, buildings, stores, signs).
- Compare answers as a class.

Answer Key

Answers will vary. Sentences could include: There are bicycles on the road. There is a moped. There is an elephant. There are two people on the elephant.

Exercise D.

Alternatively, have students write false sentences about the photo, which can be corrected by the other students.

Language Function: Asking Questions to Encourage Communication

- Practice the pronunciation of these questions.
- Model the dialogs with a student. Emphasize appropriate intonation and pronunciation.
- Pair students to practice the dialogs.

IDEAS FOR ... Expansion

- Bring in a photo of a busy street scene such as the one on this page.
- Have students look at the photo for two minutes.
- Then turn the photo over and tell them to write as many sentences as possible about it using *there is* and *there are*. Set a time limit of two minutes.

Exploring Spoken English
(page 50)

Exercise A.

- Allow time for students to write their sentences individually. They should choose a question from the Language Function box on the previous page.
- Monitor students' work for grammatical errors.
- Review any common grammar problems as a class.

Answer Key

Answers will vary.

Exercise B.

- Model one dialog with a student, emphasizing appropriate intonation for showing interest.
- Have students practice in pairs. They can change partners two or three times to practice again.
- Encourage students to continue each conversation, using their own ideas.

Exercise C. | Critical Thinking

- Model a conversation on the first topic.
- Encourage students to give reasons for their opinions.
- Monitor groups to make sure all members are participating in the conversation.

Speaking *(page 51)*

30-45 mins

Choosing the Best Idea

Exercise A.

- Read the problem aloud.
- Ask students to explain the word *pollution* and give examples of different types of pollution and its causes.
- Tell students to describe the photos and headings and try to predict how they can help to reduce pollution.
- Have students read the article to find out if their predictions were right.

Exercise B. | Critical Thinking

- Tell students to think of pros and cons for each idea.
- You may want to list these on the board.
- Ask students to explain the reasons for the choice of the best idea. You may want to develop this into a list of criteria for the best idea.

> ### IDEAS FOR . . . Checking Comprehension
>
> Ask these additional questions about the reading passage or write them on the board.
>
> 1. Which idea(s) will save people money? (1, 4, and possibly 3)
> 2. Which idea(s) will encourage people to help each other? (3)
> 3. Which idea(s) will make it more difficult to park? (2)
> 4. Which idea(s) will cost the city the most money? (1 and 4)
> 5. Which idea(s) will reduce the number of cars on the road? (all)

Exercise C. | Collaboration

- As a class, think of one or two examples.
- With a partner, students need to come up with as many ideas as possible. Each pair can make a list.

Exercise D. | Presentation

- If there is time, have groups present their ideas to the class.
- Take a class vote on the three best ideas.

> **TIP** When students give an opinion, encourage them to always give a reason to support it. This will help them reflect on their criteria for evaluation and will help develop their speaking as well as their writing skills.

> ### IDEAS FOR . . . Expansion
>
> - Have students work in groups to create a poster to persuade people to reduce pollution caused by transportation in their city.
> - They can illustrate their poster with pictures, drawings, charts, diagrams, or cartoons.
> - Display the posters on the wall in the classroom.

Viewing: Indian Railways

30 mins

(pages 52–53)

Overview of the Video

The video describes some interesting information about the railways in India.

WARM-UP

Ask students what they know about India. What is the capital, and what are the major cities? What are the important sights? What do they know of its history?

Before Viewing

Exercise A. | Prior Knowledge

Have students discuss the questions. For question 4, you may want to suggest they imagine explaining how to use the trains to a person visiting from another country. *(How do you buy a ticket? Are there different types of ticket? What do the stations look like?)*

Answer Key

Answers will vary.

Exercise B. | Using a Dictionary

Check the pronunciation of these words if necessary.

Answer Key

1. c 2. g 3. a 4. b 5. f 6. e 7. d

Exercise C. | Predicting Content

- Ask students to read the paragraph and guess the answers.
- Emphasize that there are no correct answers at this stage. (They will check their predictions when watching the video.)

Answer Key

1. rush hour 2. stressful 3. railways 4. impressive 5. rural 6. staff 7. miniature

While Viewing

Exercise A.

- Play the video.
- Check the answers by asking students to read out a sentence each.

Exercise B.

- Give time for students to read the statements before watching again.
- Play the entire video and have students compare answers.
- Write the answers on the board.

Answer Key

1. 19th century 2. 1853 3. 1929 4. Now

IDEAS FOR . . . Checking Comprehension

Ask students to define the following terms from the video. Write the terms on the board and play the video again as students figure out their meaning in this context.

rush hour, the British, steam train, track, rural villages, staff, minister, porter, performance artist, second-class carriage

---

Exercise C.

- Give students time to read through the answer choices before watching again.
- Play the video again.
- Ask students which facts they find most surprising. Which aspects of Indian Railways are the same in their country, and which are different?

Answer Key

1. train 2. crowded 3. passengers 4. stations

After Viewing

Exercise A. | Discussion

- Assign groups to discuss the questions. Each group can appoint a secretary and a spokesperson.
- Call on the spokesperson from each group to present the most interesting ideas to the class.

Exercise B. | Critical Thinking

It may be interesting for students to choose two different countries and compare how transportation has developed in each one.

Building Vocabulary
(page 54)

track 1-26

Exercise A. | Using a Dictionary

- Model the pronunciation or play the audio of each word with students repeating.
- Ask which words they know, but don't discuss the meanings yet, as this will come up in exercise **B**.

Vocabulary Note

You may want to compare miles and kilometers. (1 km is 0.62 miles.)

track 1-27

Exercise B. | Meaning from Context

- Get students' reactions to the photos and descriptions. Have they heard of any of these types of transportation before?
- Play the audio as students read the article.
- Find out which mode of transport they would like to try.

Vocabulary Note

Explain the meaning of *in record time*. (= very fast) (Remind students of *set a record* from Unit 1.)

Exercise C.

- Allow time for students to work individually.
- Ask students to tell you the answers as you write them on the board.

Answer Key

1. c 2. h 3. f 4. e 5. g 6. a 7. d 8. b

IDEAS FOR . . . Checking Comprehension

Ask these additional questions about the information in the reading, or write them on the board and have students discuss them in pairs.

1. What is the main advantage of each type of transport?
2. How might they be useful for different types of journeys or trips?
3. Why is it important to develop new modes of transportation?

Using Vocabulary
(page 55)

Exercise A.

- Do the first sentence as an example.
- Check the answers by asking volunteers to read the sentences aloud.

Answer Key

1. modern 2. get around 3. lie down 4. destination
5. old-fashioned 6. machine 7. take it easy
8. miles per hour

Exercise B. | Discussion

- Have students discuss these questions with a partner.
- Call on volunteers to tell the class their answers.
- For question 1, it may be interesting to compare which are the most relaxing forms of transportation.

Exercise C. | Critical Thinking

- Start by discussing the definition of a *modern vehicle*.
- Explain that *pros* are arguments in favor of something, and *cons* are arguments against something.
- You may want to assign a different type of vehicle to each group. (For example: *car (electric or hybrid), plane, high-speed train*.)
- As a follow-up, ask what would happen if we did not have one of these modes of transport.

Answer Key

Answers will vary.

Developing Listening Skills

(page 56–57)

45 mins

Before Listening

Exercise A. | Using a Dictionary

Ask in what situations you would wear a *helmet,* or a *safety belt.* When would you *glide* or *roll*?

Exercise B.

- Allow time for students to work individually.
- Check the answers as you write them on the board.

> **Answer Key**
>
> **1.** glide **2.** safety belt **3.** helmet **4.** favorite **5.** amazing **6.** roll

Exercise C. | Prior Knowledge

Ask students to look at the photos and guess what kinds of transportation are shown and from which countries. (Answers are shown at bottom of page.)

Listening: A Conversation

track **1-28**

Exercise A. | Listening for the Main Idea

- Play the audio. Then compare answers as a class.
- If there is disagreement, play the audio again before checking the answers

> **Answer Key**
>
> **3.** Jen's favorite parts of her trip

track **1-28**

Exercise B. | Listening for Details

- Allow time for students to complete the chart as fully as they can.
- Play the audio again.
- Draw the chart on the board and have students tell you what to write in each column.

> **Answer Key**
>
> Order of answers will vary. Zorb column: ball, roll, land or water, New Zealand, get inside. Zip Line column: glide, cable, top of the trees, safety belt, jump off, Costa Rica, climb up.

After Listening

Exercise A. | Discussion

- Have students form groups to discuss the questions.
- Remind students to use the new words from this lesson.
- Ask a volunteer from each group to summarize some of the most interesting answers from their group.

Exercise B. | Critical Thinking

- Discuss the data shown in the bar chart. What could some other causes have been?
- Have students work in groups to list the positive and negative effects of tourism on a country's economy and on the natural environment.

> **Answer Key**
>
> Answers will vary.

> **IDEAS FOR . . . Checking Comprehension**
>
> Ask students to draw a diagram to illustrate each of these methods of travel and label it with the correct words from this lesson.

> **IDEAS FOR . . . Expansion**
>
> Ask students to role-play a conversation between a representative of the Tree Top zip line company and an environmentalist. They should debate whether their company helps or harms the environment.

30 mins

Exploring Spoken English
(pages 58–59)

Grammar: *Like to, Want to, Need to*

- Illustrate the different meanings of *like, want,* and *need* with example sentences relating to the previous topic. (For example: *I like to try exciting sports. I want to go to Costa Rica. I need to save money for my next trip.*)

- Explain that these verbs can be followed by a noun (for example: *I need some new hiking shoes.*) or by a verb in the infinitive form (*to* + the base form of the verb).

> **IDEAS FOR . . . Presenting Grammar**
>
> Draw a chart on the board with three columns, one each for *like, want,* and *need.*
>
> Ask students to write three verbs in each column to describe things they *like to do, want to do,* or *need to do.*
>
> Then have them make conversations with their partner.
>
> Example:
> **A:** I want to learn how to snowboard.
> **B:** Do you want to take lessons?
> **A:** No, I don't need to take lessons because my brother likes to snowboard and he can teach me.

Exercise A.

Have volunteers write their answers on the board.

> **Answer Key**
>
> 1. She wants to ride her bicycle.
> 2. They need to wear a safety belt.
> 3. Does he like to take the bus?
> 4. I don't want to ride in a Zorb.
> 5. Do I need to wear a helmet?
> 6. She doesn't like to fly.
> 7. She wants to ride in a jet pack.
> 8. They need to walk to school.

Exercise B. | Critical Thinking

- Review the key words for showing sequence.
- Practice the sentences orally before students write.
- Monitor students' work as they write, and address any common errors.

> **Answer Key**
>
> 1. First, you need to wear a long-sleeved shirt and long pants.
> 2. Second, you need to wear sports shoes.
> 3. Third, you need to wear a helmet.
> 4. Fourth, you need to wear a safety belt and harness.

Language Function: Encouraging

- Practice saying these expressions using appropriate encouraging intonation.

- You may want to contrast intonation that is flat and not encouraging with a lively upbeat intonation that is encouraging.

Student to Student: Saying Thanks

Discuss different ways of saying thank you. *(Thanks! Thank you! That's kind of you! You're so nice!)*

Exercise A.

- Model the conversations with a student, or ask two students to model them.
- Give feedback on expression and intonation.
- Monitor students as they practice in pairs.

> **Answer Key**
>
> Answers will vary.

Exercise B.

- Make a list of vehicles on the board, including some unusual ones. For example, *hot-air balloon, kayak, dogsled.*

- As an example, choose one vehicle and ask for two or three suggestions for how to be safe in that vehicle. Tell each pair to choose one vehicle.

- Tell students to list as many ideas as possible.

> **Answer Key**
>
> Answers will vary.

Exercise C.

Encourage students to respond with additional questions.

> **IDEAS FOR . . . Expansion**
>
> Ask students to choose an activity or sport that they are experts in. Have students work in pairs to create a conversation between a person who wants to learn that sport or activity and the expert who tells them what they need to do.

45
mins

Engage: Giving a Group Presentation *(page 60)*

WARM-UP

- Bring in photos of different types of modern vehicles.
- Spread them out on a table and gather students around to discuss them and explain which ones they like and why.

Exercise A. | Brainstorming

- Have student form groups.
- Explain that each group will invent a new type of vehicle.
- Have students list their ideas on a large piece of paper. (For example, *an electric-powered air balloon, a solar-powered train.*)

TIP It is often a good idea to have students work in groups with students they don't normally sit with. One way to switch students around is to give each student a number or a letter in sequence. For example, number every student consecutively 1, 2, 3, or 4. Then ask everyone to stand up. Ask all 1s to sit together, all 2s to sit together, and so on.

Exercise B. | Organizing Details

- Have students choose the best idea in their group and fill out the chart.
- Walk around and provide help as needed.

Exercise C. | Planning a Presentation

- Explain that in a group presentation, each member of the group will present one part of the presentation. They can help each other prepare what they are going to say. Members should speak for roughly equal amounts of time.
- Have students practice in their groups.

Presentation Skills: Introducing Your Group

- Read the information in the box.
- Read the example, emphasizing speaking clearly, pausing, and making eye contact with the class.
- Ask three or four students to model similar examples using the names in their group.

Exercise D. | Presentation

- Invite groups to come to the front of the class and give their presentations.
- Encourage the rest of the class to ask questions after each presentation.
- Remind students to give positive feedback and encouragement.
- Give feedback on these presentation skills: introducing the group, content and organization of ideas, speaking clearly, making eye contact, and asking for questions.

TIP To help students develop confidence before giving their presentations, you may ask them to present to another group first before presenting to the class.

IDEAS FOR . . . Expansion

For homework, have students do some research about new developments in transportation. They can present the information—with pictures or diagrams if possible—in the next class.

Unusual Destinations

Academic Pathways

Lesson A: Listening to a Presentation
                  Choosing the Best Vacation

Lesson B: Listening to a Group Conversation
                  Giving an Individual Presentation

Unit Theme

Unit 4 explores the topic of unusual travel destinations, including places that are natural and those that are manmade.

Think and Discuss *(page 61)*

5 mins

- Ask students to describe what is special or unusual about the photo. Find out if anyone knows what the Northern Lights are or what causes them.

- Discuss what students know about countries in the Arctic Circle, or about people or animals in this part of the world.

- Explain that some people visit Norway just to see the Northern Lights. What makes them so fascinating?

Note: The *Northern Lights* are a natural phenomenon occurring in the skies above the magnetic North Pole. They are bright green, pink, yellow, or red dancing lights or curtains of light and are caused by collisions between electrically charged particles from the sun that enter the earth's atmosphere. They are known as "Aurora borealis" in the north and "Aurora australis" in the south.

Exploring the Theme

15 mins

(pages 62–63)

The opening spread features two unusual vacation destinations: underwater caves in the Bahamas and caves in Turkey.

- Ask students to describe the two photos. What are the colors, shapes, or sounds? What is the atmosphere like?

- Review the locations of the Bahamas and Turkey, pointing them out on a map, if available.

- Read the information about unusual vacations. Find out if students agree with these statements.

- Discuss question 1. Survey the class to find out if more students choose the same destination over and over or prefer to visit new places. Or, if students don't travel much, find out what are some typical travel destinations for people in their city or country.

- Discuss question 2. Compare the photos using different criteria: size, color, manmade, natural, easy or difficult to access, historic, a good place to live, or to see wildlife.

- Discuss question 3. Take a class vote. Discuss pros and cons of visiting each place.

Vocabulary Note

Stalactites and stalagmites are found in limestone caves. They are formed by slightly acidic water dripping down and dissolving the limestone. Stalactites hang downwards from the roof of the cave. Stalagmites point upwards and are formed by drips falling from the stalactite. They sometimes join to form columns.

IDEAS FOR . . . **Expansion**

Bring in pictures of unusual places to visit from magazines or vacation brochures. Form groups and give each group a few photos or brochures. Each group must choose one destination they would like to visit and then explain to the other groups the reasons for their choice.

Building Vocabulary

(page 64)

30 mins

WARM-UP

The Lesson A target vocabulary is presented in the context of unusual vacation destinations.

- Ask students about what kind of vacations they like and why.
- Ask students to describe the most unusual vacation destination they have ever visited.

Exercise A. | Using a Dictionary

track 1-29

- Play the audio and have students repeat each word (optional).
- Correct pronunciation or stress if necessary.
- Tell students to check the words they are already familiar with before they look up new words.

Exercise B. | Meaning from Context

track 1-30

- Ask students to describe the picture. They may remember the word *glacier* from unit 1.
- Ask why they think people would like to visit this place.
- Play the audio as students listen and read along, paying special attention to the words in blue.

Answer Key

1. breathtaking **2.** relax **3.** unusual **4.** secluded
5. to get away **6.** vacation **7.** unknown **8.** spot

- Allow time for students to complete their answers individually.
- Model the correct pronunciation of any difficult words, or play the audio from exercise **A**.

IDEAS FOR . . . Checking Comprehension

Ask additional questions about the text or write them on the board.

1. What is similar about these two places? (They are quiet and not crowded.)
2. What is different about them? (The first is probably hot and you can swim. The second is extremely cold and you have to wear warm clothes.)
3. Why do they think these places are not crowded? (They are difficult to get to. Not many tourists know about them.)

Using Vocabulary

(page 65)

30 mins

Exercise A.

- Ask students to look at the picture and describe what this man is doing. Useful vocabulary: *beach, sun bed, sun umbrella, sunbathe.*
- Do the first item as an example.
- Allow time for students to complete their answers individually.
- Choose two students to read the conversation out loud. Make sure others in the class agree on the answers.
- Ask who these two speakers are, where they are, and what they are doing.

Answer Key

1. vacation **2.** unknown **3.** spots **4.** secluded
5. breathtaking **6.** get away **7.** relax

Exercise B.

- Pair students to read the conversation, then switch roles and read it again.
- Monitor students as they practice and give tips on pronunciation. Focus on correct pronunciation of the new words and natural intonation and expression.
- Ask volunteers to present their conversations to the class.

TIP As an extension, have students make up their own conversations using as many of these words as they can. You could have a competition to see who can include the most words.

Exercise C. | Discussion

- Give your own answers to a couple of these questions as examples.
- Pair students to discuss their answers.
- Remind students to try and use the target words in their answers.
- Ask volunteers to summarize their answers for each question and present them to the class.

Developing Listening Skills

45 mins *(pages 66–67)*

Before Listening

Using Visuals to Activate Prior Knowledge

Discuss the information in the box. What other kinds of visuals can a speaker use? (For example: diagrams, drawings, charts.) Why is it a good idea to use visuals? (It activates visual intelligence and helps to make spoken and written information clearer and more interesting.)

Exercise A. | Understanding Visuals

- Point out and name the different types of visuals in exercise **A**, and discuss how they make the information clearer and prepare you for the information to come in the presentation. (For example: The different colored arrows and boxes pointing to the map and the photos show the relationships between them.)
- Play the audio. Tell students to refer to the visuals as they listen.
- Give students time to read the sentences and write their answers.
- Check the answers as a class and tell students to identify which parts of the visuals helped them to find the answers.

Exercise B. | Prior Knowledge

- Partners should share information about these countries either using their own knowledge or from the visuals.
- You may ask some questions such as, *What are rice paddies? What is special about Nepal? What is the capital city of Thailand? What is the sea between China and the Philippines?*

Listening: A Presentation

track 1-31

Exercise A. | Listening for Main Ideas

- As an optional starter activity, you may want to tell students to write three things they expect to hear in the presentation.
- Ask students to read the questions.
- Play the audio while students circle their answers.
- Compare answers as a class.

track 1-31

Exercise B. | Listening for Details

- Have students read the statements.
- Play the audio again. Then pair students to compare their answers.
- Play the audio or sections of the audio again if necessary.
- Ask students' opinions about the presentation. What did they find interesting or surprising?

> **IDEAS FOR ...** Checking Comprehension
>
> Ask these additional questions or write them on the board.
>
> 1. What does Tom say about secluded beaches in Thailand? (They are peaceful and relaxing.)
> 2. What does Tom say about the Himalayas? (They are serene and the views are spectacular.)
> 3. What does he hope his pictures will do? (Inspire other people to travel to unknown places.)

After Listening

Critical Thinking

- For question 1, ask students to explain what each book might be about.
- For question 2, tell students to come up with as many different meanings as possible.
- Ask students if they have read any travel books. Which book would they recommend to the others in the class and why?

Note: Robert Frost (1874–1963) was a well-known American poet. This poem is one of his best known and is often studied in school. It has been interpreted in many different ways. One interpretation is that it is good to follow one's spirit of adventure and not be afraid of trying something new. Another is that whichever path you choose, it is individual and unique to you. A third interpretation is that whichever path you choose, you cannot go back.

Exploring Spoken English

45 mins

(pages 68–69)

Grammar: The Present Continuous

- Highlight the difference in meaning between the present continuous and the simple present.

- Ask questions about the form of the present continuous. What is the word order? Why does the verb *be* change? Does the *-ing* verb change? How are contractions formed?

- Review the spelling rules for adding the *-ing* ending. For example: writing (drop *e*), swimming (double a final consonant after a single vowel).

> **IDEAS FOR . . . Presenting Grammar**
>
> Prepare some cards or slips of paper with a variety of different actions on them that are easy to mime. Pass one out to each pair of students. Student A mimes the action on the card. Student B tries to guess what they are doing. When they are done, they can pass their card on to another pair.
>
> Examples:
> You are eating a sandwich.
> You are swimming in the ocean.
> You are reading a magazine.
> You are answering your email.
> You are texting a friend.
> You are taking a picture.

Exercise A.

- Read the first example together with the class.

- Make sure that students understand the concept by asking questions. Is she eating breakfast right now? (Yes, she is.) Does she eat breakfast on the balcony every day? (We don't know.) Did she do this yesterday? (We don't know.)

- Allow time for students to write their answers.

- Call on volunteers to come to the board and write their answers.

Answer Key

Answers will vary, but should be similar to the following:

It's now 8:00 A.M., and I am eating breakfast on my balcony.

It's now 11:00 A.M., and we are riding bicycles on the beach.

It's now 2:00 P.M., and I am relaxing/reading on the beach.

It's now 4:00 P.M., and I am riding on a boat.

Exercise B.

- Tell students to think about what is happening in the photo.

- Allow time for students to complete the conversation. Remind them to make sure to use the correct form of the verb *be*.

- Check the answers and write them on the board before students practice in pairs.

- Make sure students use contracted forms, as this is a conversation.

Answer Key

1. am looking **2.** am riding **3.** are riding **4.** are walking
5. is driving **6.** are hiking **7.** are resting **8.** are smiling
9. are having

Exercise C.

- Ask students to name things in the picture (*camel, desert, tourists, tour guide*).

- Have students work individually to write sentences.

Answer Key

Answers will vary.

Language Function: Asking For Repetition

- Model the questions and ask students to repeat.

- Emphasize appropriate intonation and pronunciation.

- Model how to use these questions by asking a student: *What are you doing?* Then ask them to repeat by using one of these expressions.

> **IDEAS FOR . . . Expansion**
>
> - Bring in pictures of scenes from different countries that show people engaged in different activities.
> - Distribute the pictures to pairs or have each pair choose one.
> - Students write six sentences, three true and three false, using the present continuous.
> - They pass their paper and their picture to another pair.
> - The next pair will identify the true and the false sentences.

Exploring Spoken English
(page 70)

track 1-32

Exercise A.

- Play the audio while students read.
- If appropriate, play the audio and pause after each sentence so that students can repeat using correct pronunciation and intonation.

Answer Key

Conversation 1
A: What are you doing?
B: I'm reading a book on South Africa.
A: What did you say?
B: I'm reading a book on South Africa. I'm going to Cape Town next month.

Conversation 2
A: Do you want to have dinner now?
B: No, I'm planning my vacation.
A: Did you say you're planning your vacation?
B: Yes, I leave next week!

Exercise B.

- Have students practice in pairs. They can change partners two or three times to practice again.
- Tell students to continue each conversation using their own ideas.

Exercise C. | Critical Thinking

- Read the examples. Make sure students know that they should not say the name of the place, only the activities they are doing there.
- Give an additional example by saying a few sentences about what you are doing in your own favorite vacation place.
- Alternatively, you can distribute cards with names or pictures of vacation places to use in this activity.

Critical Thinking Focus: Describing

- To illustrate this point, you may want to contrast an example of a description with few details, and one with many details.
- You can also use one of the pictures in this unit (such as page 62 or page 64) and ask students for ideas for details that could be included in a description: colors, shapes, sounds, atmosphere.

Speaking *(page 71)*

30-45 mins

Choosing the Best Vacation

Exercise A.

- Ask students to describe the pictures, including as many details as they can.
- Go over the words in the box and answer any questions about meaning.
- To check comprehension, ask students to give examples of vacations that correspond with each adjective.
- Allow time for students to complete the chart.
- Draw the chart on the board. Choose three volunteers to come and complete the chart with information from the rest of the class.

Answer Key

Answers will vary.

Exercise B. | Critical Thinking

Encourage students to think of reasons and details to support their arguments. They may want to make notes.

Exercise C.

Tell students to think of reasons and details to support their arguments. They may want to make notes.

Exercise D. | Collaboration

Students can ask you questions about your likes and dislikes to help with this task.

Exercise E. | Presentation

After each pair presents their ideas, make your selection and give reasons for your choice.

IDEAS FOR ... **Expansion**

- Students work in groups.
- Give each student a name or a picture of a vacation destination.
- Each student will list the advantages of their place and try to persuade the others in their group to go there.
- Finally, the group will choose the best vacation.
- Ask a spokesperson from each group to tell the class and explain the reasons for their choice.

Viewing: Blue Lagoon
(pages 72–73)

30 mins

Overview of the Video

The video is about a geothermal lagoon in Iceland where people go to swim and rest because of the relaxing and medicinal qualities of the water.

WARM-UP

Find out what students know about Iceland and spas.

Before Viewing

Exercise A. | Prior Knowledge

Draw the diagram on the board and write all the words that students come up with around the diagram.

Answer Key

Answers will vary.

Exercise B. | Predicting Content

- Check that everyone understands the meaning of the word *spa*. Refer to the picture and explain that it is a place with natural mineral water (hot or warm) that people believe will make you healthy if you bathe in it.
- Ask if anyone has ever been to a spa. Where was it? What was it like? What therapies did it offer?
- Allow time for students to complete the chart.
- Emphasize that there are no correct answers at this stage. They will review the chart after watching the video.

Answer Key

Answers will vary.

Exercise C. | Using a Dictionary

Tell students to match the words and definitions. Then they can use their dictionaries to check any they are unsure of.

Answer Key

1. g 2. d 3. a 4. f 5. b 6. e 7. c

While Viewing

Exercise A. | Checking Predictions

Tell students to look back at exercise B on the previous page and say which of their predictions were correct.

Exercise B.

Give students time to read all the questions before watching the video again.

Answer Key

1. [4] The water goes into the lava fields. [3] The plant pumps the water back out. [2] The plant uses the water to make energy. [5] The water forms a lagoon. [1] The power plant takes super heated water out of the ground. 2. b 3. b 4. c

---

IDEAS FOR . . . Checking Comprehension

Ask these additional questions or write them on the board.

1. What color is the rock? (black)
2. What color is the water? (blue, milky, aquamarine)
3. What is in the water? (blue-green algae)
4. What is at the bottom of the lagoon? (white silica mud)
5. What do people do with the mud? (They spread it over their bodies to make their skin soft and cure skin ailments.)

Exercise C. | Using the Present Continuous

- Press the mute button and play the video again, pausing as appropriate.
- Pair students to describe activities in the video.
- Choose one or two scenes from the video and have students describe them to you.

After Viewing

Exercise A. | Discussion

Remind students to use the vocabulary words in blue in their discussion.

Exercise B. | Critical Thinking

It may be interesting for students to role-play a conversation between two people taking opposing points of view on this topic.

Building Vocabulary

30 mins

(page 74)

Exercise A. | Meaning from Context

track 1-33

- Point out the photos and read the headings. Ask what they already know about each of these places.
- Play the audio while students read.
- Ask some easy comprehension questions. For example: *Which ones are modern? Which ones are old? Why were these places created?*

Exercise B.

- Have students match the words and the definitions.
- Write the answers on the board.

> **TIP** As extra practice, ask students to work in pairs. Student A covers exercise B. Student B reads a definition and student A finds the target word in the text.

> **Answer Key**
>
> 1. e 2. f 3. g 4. h 5. d 6. c 7. b 8. a

> **IDEAS FOR . . . Checking Comprehension**
>
> Ask these additional questions about the information in the reading or write them on the board and have students discuss them in pairs.
>
> 1. What do these places have in common?
> 2. What is unique about each place?
> 3. Which place would they most like to visit and why?

Using Vocabulary

(page 75)

Exercise A.

- Ask students to describe the photo.
- Do the first sentence as an example.
- Allow time for students to work individually.
- Check the answers by calling on volunteers to read the sentences aloud.

> **Answer Key**
>
> 1. attractions 2. view 3. natural 4. overlooks
> 5. manmade 6. recommends 7. mix 8. spectacular

Exercise B. | Discussion.

As additional points, you may want to discuss these questions: *What makes a place or a building beautiful? What makes a city ugly or beautiful? Do different cultures have different ideas about the beauty of natural or manmade landscapes?*

Exercise C. | Critical Thinking

- Start by brainstorming one place for each category.
- You may want to write some useful vocabulary on the board as they come up. For example: manmade: *palace, mosque, cathedral, tower, dam, bridge, aqueduct;* natural: *coral reef, canyon, desert, glacier, fjord, volcano, geyser.*
- Draw the chart on the board and ask volunteers to come to the board to write their ideas. You may want to take a class vote on the most impressive attraction in each category.

> **Answer Key**
>
> Answers will vary.

Exercise D.

As a follow-up, ask students to bring in pictures of places they have visited and tell the class about it in the next lesson.

Developing Listening Skills
(pages 76–77)

45 mins

Before Listening

Predicting Content

- Ask students to describe the picture. What is strange or unusual about it? Why might people want to go there? Who might want to stay there?

- Write some ideas and useful vocabulary on the board.

- Useful vocabulary: *cave, igloo, ice, benches, furs, animal skins, arches, carved.*

Listening: A Group Conversation

Exercise A. | Checking Predictions

track 1-34

- Play the audio. What kind of place is it?

- Together with the class, check which ideas on the board were mentioned on the audio.

- If there is disagreement, wait to resolve it until after playing the audio again.

Exercise B. | Listening for the Main Idea

track 1-34

- Play the audio again.

- Check the answer and also check any previous predictions that were not clear.

Answer Key

b. It was a good mix of a natural and manmade attraction.

Exercise C. | Listening for Details

track 1-34

- Allow time for students to read the sentences.

- Play the audio again.

- Check the answers and ask students to correct any false sentences.

Answer Key

The following details should be circled:
It's 200 km north of the Arctic Circle.

You sleep on reindeer skins.

There were 47 rooms this year.

The temperature stays between –5 and –8 degrees Celsius.

They serve you hot juice in the morning.

Exercise D. | Making Inferences

track 1-34

- Check that students understand the meaning of the word *inference*. (Students have to draw a conclusion about something that is not directly stated.)

- Allow time for students to read the sentences.

- Play the audio again.

- Check the answers and have students correct any false sentences.

Answer Key

1. F 2. T 3. T 4. T

Exercise E.

- Discuss the answers as a class. Ask students to explain how they reached their conclusions.

- Ask students to correct any false sentences.

- Discuss whether students would like to stay at the ICEHOTEL. Why or why not?

After Listening

Collaboration

- Discuss what makes the ICEHOTEL a successful tourist attraction. What are its unique characteristics? How does it appeal to people? What kinds of sales and marketing techniques might be used to advertise it?

- Students may work individually to complete the chart. Alternatively, they may want to brainstorm some ideas in their group. Then choose one idea to work on in detail.

- Ask a volunteer from each group to tell the class about the most interesting idea from their group.

Answer Key

Answers will vary.

Pronunciation: Reduction of *-ing*

track 1-35

- Explain that understanding fast speech is useful for listening skills as well as for pronunciation.

- Play the audio with students repeating each sentence.

- Say one of the sentences and have students tell you if it is careful or fast speech.

- Give feedback while students are practicing in pairs.

IDEAS FOR . . . Checking Comprehension

Ask these additional questions about the audio or write them on the board and have students discuss them in pairs.

1. Describe how the ICEHOTEL is constructed. (Snow builders and artists from around the world make the hotel. They spray snow onto steel walls, and, after they freeze, they take the walls away and the snow walls stay up.)
2. Describe where and how you sleep. (In a warm sleeping bag on a special bed of snow, ice, and reindeer skins.)
3. What can you see around the hotel? (There is spectacular ice art all around the hotel.)

IDEAS FOR . . . Expansion

Students can role-play a conversation between a representative of the ICEHOTEL and a tour organizer. The ICEHOTEL representative should try to persuade the tour organizer to bring tourists to visit the hotel.

Exploring Spoken English
(pages 78–79)

30 mins

Grammar: The Present Continuous in Questions

▨ Tell students to notice the word order in *Yes/No* and *Wh*-questions. (In yes/no questions, the verb comes first.)

▨ Model the questions, paying special attention to stress and intonation, with students repeating.

▨ Remind students of spelling rules for -*ing* forms.

IDEAS FOR . . . Presenting Grammar

Bring in pictures of people (or ask students to choose a photo from a previous unit in this book) and ask each pair to make 10 questions about it using the present continuous. Then have each pair ask the class their questions while other students in the class try to answer them. Give feedback on grammar and pronunciation as well as creative ideas.

Exercise A.

Allow time for students to complete their answers individually.

Answer Key

1. Are you planning your trip to Easter Island?
2. Where is your brother going on vacation?
3. Are your parents getting away?
4. Why is John going to a secluded spot?
5. Are your friends riding the train?
6. When is the plane coming?
7. Are you leaving now?
8. Are my friends relaxing on the beach now?

 track 1-36

Exercise B.

▨ Play the audio.

▨ Ask students to tell you the present continuous forms.

▨ You may want to play the audio and have students repeat either as a class or individually.

▨ Draw students' attention to the stress, rhythm, and intonation and have them try to keep the same speed as the audio.

Note: The photo shows one of the mysterious giant statues *(moai)* on Easter Island in the Pacific Ocean. No one knows exactly why these statues were created or how they were transported.

Answer Key

A: Hi, Keiko? <u>Are you working now</u>?
B: No, <u>I'm taking my vacation</u> this week.
A: Where are you?
B: I'm on Easter Island. I'm on a group tour with 15 other people.
A: Wow! <u>Are you having a good time</u>?
B: Yes, <u>I'm learning</u> a lot about the island, and <u>I'm having a lot of fun</u>.
A: <u>What are you doing right now</u>?
B: <u>I'm hiking up a big mountain</u>.
A: <u>Are you seeing beautiful views</u>?
B: Yes, <u>I'm standing on a bridge</u> that overlooks the island's famous statues. It's a spectacular view!

Exercise C.

Monitor students and give feedback as they practice in pairs.

Exercise D. | Role-Playing

▨ Read the instructions and check that students understand by asking questions. *Who are you talking to? Where are you? What are you talking about?*

▨ Allow time for pairs to complete the conversation. Remind them to use the present continuous.

▨ Encourage students to choose interesting and unusual places for their imaginary vacations.

■ Ask volunteers to perform the conversation for the class. Praise interesting content, good vocabulary, as well as natural pronunciation and intonation.

Student to Student: Working Together

Discuss the importance of working together in teams and groups in classrooms and in workplaces.

Exercise E. | Discussion

■ Brainstorm ideas for different types of vacations: single, with another person, with a group from work or school, with your family, and briefly discuss which ones are better and why.

■ For the second question, make sure everyone understands the meaning of *group tour* (= a tour organized by a tour company where groups of people travel together for a week or longer with a tour guide on a fixed itinerary).

Answer Key

Answers will vary.

IDEAS FOR . . . Expansion

Ask students to use the chart to make a short presentation on this topic. They may practice using these phrases:

There are several reasons for taking a group tour. First . . . Second . . . Third . . .

On the other hand, there are also some reasons against taking a group tour. First . . . Second . . . Third . . .

Engage: Giving an Individual Presentation *(page 80)*

45 mins

WARM-UP

■ Bring in pictures of different types of vacation destinations.

■ Spread them out on a table and gather students around to discuss them and say which ones they like and why.

■ Alternatively, pin the pictures on the wall around the classroom and have students walk around and choose the one they like best. They can then sit in pairs and explain the reasons for their choice to their partner.

Exercise A. | Critical Thinking

■ Read the task aloud.

■ Explain that each student will give their own presentation.

■ Discuss the three photos and say what you can do in each place. (1. visit pyramids, visit museums, and temples; 2. sit on the beach, swim, sunbathe, relax; 3. go hiking, climbing, caving, camping.)

■ Ask questions about the example pie chart. What does this person like most/least?

■ Allow time for students to complete their own pie chart.

TIP One way to practice gaining confidence in giving a presentation is to have students record their own voice while giving a presentation. Then they can play back the recording and think about how to improve their presentation skills.

Exercise B. | Planning a Presentation

■ Read aloud the example presentation.

■ Emphasize speaking clearly, pausing, and making eye contact. Make sure to hold up the visual and point to it while you are speaking.

■ Allow time for students to write their own similar presentation.

■ You may want to mention that in a real presentation, it is more usual to speak from notes.

Exercise C. | Practicing Your Presentation

■ Explain that the visual should be large enough for all the class members to see it clearly.

■ You may want to provide large pieces of paper for the graphics.

Presentation Skills: Using Graphics

■ Read the information in the box.

■ Discuss the importance of using graphics.

■ Demonstrate how to use these phrases while pointing.

■ Ask one or two students to read the relevant sentences from the example presentation while holding up the book and pointing to the graphic.

Exercise D. | Presentation

■ Tell the class to ask questions after each presentation.

■ Give feedback on speaking clearly, making eye contact, and using graphics.

Our Changing World

Academic Pathways

Lesson A: Listening to a Lecture
              Discussing Traditions

Lesson B: Listening to a Short Documentary
              Presenting to a Small Group

Unit Theme

Unit 5 explores the topic of how our world is changing and how traditions are disappearing.

Think and Discuss *(page 81)*

5 mins

- Point out the unit title and the Academic Pathways at the top of the page. These items will give students a preview of the unit.

- Discuss the questions. Ask students to suggest possible answers to these questions. *Why is the man standing on a rock? Why did he choose to build his retreat on top of a mountain? What is the possible significance of the rock and the tree for his philosophy?* Find out what students know about kung fu or other ancient martial arts of China.

Vocabulary Note

retreat (n) is a place that is quiet where a person can go for meditation and prayer

Exploring the Theme

15 mins

(pages 82–83)

The opening spread features two pictures of Manhattan Island in New York. One is an artistic recreation of what it may have looked like 400 years ago. The other is a contemporary photograph.

- Point to Manhattan Island on a map. Ask what students know about the history of New York City and of Manhattan. Who settled here in the 1600s and why?

- Find out if any students have visited Manhattan. If so, have them describe it for the class. Ask these questions of the class: *What do you know about Manhattan? What is it famous for?*

- Discuss the first question as a class. Have students describe each photo in detail. Useful vocabulary: *forest, vegetation, coast, inlet, harbor, built-up, crowded, skyscrapers, docks, concrete jungle.*

- Read the second question and give an example from your life. Then pair students to discuss it and to come up with one example each of a tradition that has changed (in their family or in their culture).

- Ask volunteers to share their opinion with the class and discuss whether each change is good (or not) and why.

- Read the paragraph and discuss other changes that are taking place in society. For example, changes in technology, information systems, communication.

IDEAS FOR . . .   Expansion

Form groups and assign each group a different topic. Tell groups to brainstorm ideas about what has changed over the last 50 years in terms of the topic.

Possible topics:

Food, transportation and cars, communication, work, education, clothing, music, climate, movies, entertainment, TV, houses/apartments, lifestyle.

Example: People in the past traveled long distances by ship and train. Now they travel by airplane.

Building Vocabulary

(page 84)

30 mins

WARM-UP

The Lesson A target vocabulary is presented in the context of a kung fu school.

1. Ask students if they have ever seen a kung fu film. If so, ask them to describe it for the class.

2. If possible, show a clip from a kung fu film or training lesson from YouTube.

Exercise A. | Using a Dictionary

track 2-01

- Play the audio and have students repeat each word (optional).

- Correct pronunciation or stress if necessary.

- Give students time to look up any words they don't know.

Exercise B.

After checking the answers, ask students to make example sentences with each word.

Answer Key

1. d 2. a 3. b 4. c

Exercise C. | Meaning from Context

track 2-02

- Ask students about the photo. What are these boys doing? How do they feel? Why are they there?

- Play the audio as students read.

- Play the audio again while students write.

- Read the footnotes and check the answers as a class.

- Ask if students would like to join this school. Why, or why not?

Note: If students ask about the history of Shaolin kung fu, note that it is explained in exercise **B** on the next page.

Answer Key

1. practice 2. young 3. entertainment 4. develop

IDEAS FOR . . .   Checking Comprehension

Ask additional questions about the text or write them on the board.

1. Describe Hu Zhengsheng's personality.
2. What makes him a good student of kung fu?
3. Is 11 years old very young to be a student of kung fu?
4. Why do students sleep in cold rooms?
5. Why do they practice early in the morning?
6. What skills and qualities does the kung fu school develop in its students?

Using Vocabulary *(page 85)*

30 mins

Exercise A. | Group Discussion

- Form groups of two or three students.

- Allow time for discussion. Then ask one student from each group to summarize the answers for the class.

- Add your own opinions.

Exercise B.

track 2-03

- Ask questions about the photo. What are they doing? Who are they? Why are they fighting? What are they fighting with? Is it past or present?

- Play the audio while students read.

- Alternatively, play the audio after students have completed the blanks.

- As an extension, ask students to write three questions about the passage (using the target vocabulary, if possible).

- Write the questions on the board and have the class check them for grammatical accuracy.

Answer Key

1. practice 2. skills 3. hope 4. competitions

Exercise C.

- Pair students to complete the activity and practice the conversation.

- Choose volunteers to present their conversation to the class.

- Give feedback on pronunciation and intonation.

Answer Key

1. practice 2. young 3. competitions 4. skills

TIP   Higher-level students can try to memorize the conversation. Lower-level students can switch roles and practice the conversation again.

Developing Listening Skills

45 mins

(pages 86–87)

track 2-04

Pronunciation: Using Intonation to Ask for Something or Make a Request

- Review these different ways of making a request: *Can you . . . Could you . . . Would you mind (+ing)*, and *Will you . . . ?*

- Play the audio, with the class repeating. Then call on individuals to read the examples.

- Highlight any difficulties with intonation and pronunciation.

- Tell students to make two other requests using these forms.

- Point out that some questions rise and some fall (see pronunciation later in this unit, Lesson **B**, page 96).

> **TIP** When teaching pronunciation, it is sometimes helpful to hum the intonation pattern of a sentence to show how the pitch glides up or down. Be aware that in some cultures it is not appropriate for men to use high-pitched intonation.

- Read the example with the class and practice saying the request.

- Tell students to use a different form in each example.

- Give feedback on intonation while students practice in pairs.

Answer Key

Answers will vary, but should include the following verbs and similar phrases for making requests:
1. Will you drive me to the competition?
2. Could you tell me what time the competition starts, please?
3. Excuse me, can you teach me more about kung fu?
4. Would you mind helping me with an exercise?

Before Listening

Predicting Content

- Discuss the picture in pairs or as a class.

- Useful vocabulary: *tent, wigwam, feathers, headdress, costume, decorated, colorful.*

- Have students write three things they expect to hear in the lecture. These will be useful when you come to exercise **C** on the next page.

Listening: A Lecture

track 2-05

Exercise A. | Listening for the Main Idea

- Tell students to read the statements.

- Play the audio while students choose their answers.

- Compare answers as a class.

Answer Key

The following main idea should be checked: Traditions change over time.

track 2-05

Exercise B. | Listening for Details

- Tell students to read the statements.

- Play the audio again. Then have students compare answers in pairs.

- Ask for students' opinions about the lecture. What did they find interesting or surprising?

Answer Key

1. c 2. b 3. a

Exercise C. | Checking Predictions

track 2-05

If some are unsure whether their predictions were correct, play the audio again.

> **IDEAS FOR . . . Checking Comprehension**
>
> Ask these additional questions or write them on the board. Play the audio again.
>
> 1. List three ways in which pow-wows have changed. *(Dancing is done for money or to win competitions, new dances and songs are brought in, women play drums, people stay in hotels and eat in restaurants, non-Native Americans participate)*
> 2. List three important functions of pow-wows. *(Renew old friendships, make new friends, wear traditional clothes, eat traditional food, dance traditional dances, honor the past and celebrate the future, maintain culture and strengthen community)*

After Listening

Self-Reflection

- Brainstorm some other examples of traditional celebrations with the class. For example, Thanksgiving, midsummer solstice, Mardi Gras.

- If the partners are from different countries, have them tell each other about their traditions. If they are from the same country, ask them to list the three most important traditional celebrations and say why they are important.

Exploring Spoken English
(pages 88–89)

45 mins

Grammar: The Simple Past Tense

- Highlight the difference in meaning between the present and the past. Draw a diagram on the board if necessary.
- Explain that there are two types of verbs: regular verbs that add *-ed* in the past, and irregular verbs that change completely.
- Introduce the rules and examples in the box.

> **IDEAS FOR . . . Presenting Grammar**
>
> Practice past forms by saying the present form and asking students to say the past.
>
> Example
> **T:** like
> **S:** liked
> **T:** think
> **S:** thought
>
> Have students practice in pairs.
> Do a dictation by dictating present forms and having students write the past form of each word.

track **2-06**

- Point out the photo. What do students think the reading will be about? Useful vocabulary: *pastry, cake, dessert, bake.*
- Play the audio as students fill in the blanks.
- Alternatively, ask students to fill in the blanks. Then play the audio to check the answers.
- Call on volunteers to read the conversation aloud.

Answer Key

1. wanted 2. thought 3. helped 4. worked 5. baked
6. liked 7. learned

Language Function: Past Tense Expressions

- Stick or draw a calendar on the board.
- Point to the relevant day and ask students to identify the correct expression.
- Choose volunteers to come up to the board and do the same.
- You may want to teach additional expressions if appropriate. For example: *the day before yesterday, the day after tomorrow,* and so on.

Exercise A.

- Give some examples of your own.
- Allow time for students to complete their sentences.
- Monitor students' work as they practice in pairs.
- Give feedback on any common errors.

Answer Key

Answers will vary.

> **IDEAS FOR . . . Expansion**
>
> Give out one slip of paper to each student, each with a sentence starter such as *Yesterday . . . Last night . . . Last week . . . One week ago . . . One year ago . . . ,* and the like.
>
> Have each student write one true sentence. Then collect all the slips. Mix them up and give them out again. Then have students walk around to find the person who wrote their slip by asking questions.

track **2-07**

Exercise B.

- Discuss the photos. What is the main difference between them?
- Ask students to circle the correct time expressions. Then play the audio to check the answers.
- Have students answer the questions posed in the last lines of the paragraph.

Answer Key

1. today 2. Many years ago 3. today 4. tomorrow
5. today

Exercise C.

- Tell students to list as many differences as they can.
- Make a list on the board.
- Have students make sentences starting with *Many years ago . . . Now . . .*

Exploring Spoken English
(page 90)

Exercise D.

- Point out the location of Dubai on a world map.
- Find out what students know about it. Do they think it is modern or traditional? What traditions do they think it has?
- Allow time for students to complete the gaps.
- Play the audio while students read.
- If you think it is helpful, play the audio and pause after each sentence so that students can repeat using correct pronunciation and intonation.
- Have students practice in pairs and then change partners two or three times to practice again.

TIP For lower-level students, it may be easier if you play the audio while students fill in the blanks as they listen.

Answer Key

1. shop 2. live 3. work 4. lived 5. loved 6. enjoyed
7. noticed 8. see 9. eat 10. know

Exercise E.

- Ask students to describe the photo. Pair students to discuss the questions.
- As they write their answers, make sure they are using present and past forms correctly.

Answer Key

Answers will vary.

Exercise F. | Discussion

- If students come from the same town, have them list all the changes in their groups. If they come from different places, ask them to find out what changes all their towns or cities have in common.
- You may want to assign this as extra writing practice in their journal for homework.

Speaking *(page 91)*

30-45 mins

Discussing Traditions

Exercise A. | Self-Reflection

- Ask students to describe the picture, including as many details as they can.
- Brainstorm a few different traditions and answer the questions about one of them as an example.
- Allow time for students to complete the information about their chosen tradition.

Answer Key

Answers will vary.

Exercise B.

- For this exercise, it may be best for students to stand up and sit down with someone who has chosen a different tradition.
- Encourage students to ask additional questions to get more detailed information from their partner.

Exercise C. | Critical Thinking

Remind students to think of reasons and details to support their arguments.

IDEAS FOR . . . Expansion

Give each group the name of a traditional celebration to research for homework. Each student can research one aspect of the celebration. For example: the music, the food, the clothing, the origins, the month or season, the duration.

Have each group present their celebration to the class, and bring in photos if possible.

Examples:
Songkran, Carnival, Fasching, Midsummer, Guy Fawkes Night, Halloween, Hogmanay

---

Viewing: Pow-Wows
(pages 92–93)

30 mins

Overview of the Video

The video gives a Native American perspective on the Native American tradition of a pow-wow.

WARM-UP

Briefly discuss the photo with students. Ask what they already know (or remember) about Native American life and culture. If possible, show a map of Native American tribes in North America and talk about some of the most famous events and names in their history or describe some other aspects of their life and culture.

Before Viewing

Exercise A. | Critical Thinking

- Discuss the questions as a class.
- Discuss why some people might be against change.

Answer Key

Answers will vary.

Exercise B. | Using a Dictionary

track 2-08

- Play the audio while students read.
- Ask questions to help students figure out the meaning of the underlined words. For example: Does *reservation* mean a place, a person, or an action? Who probably taught him to dance? Does *gradually* mean slowly or quickly? Would he probably change from an old to a new style, or from a new to an old style?

Exercise C.

- Give students time to complete the activity.
- Check the answers and write them on the board.
- Discuss how accurate their guesses were in exercise **B**.

Answer Key

1. ancestors **2.** contemporary **3.** reservation
4. gradually

While Viewing

Exercise A.

- Give students time to read all the questions before watching.
- Play the video while students choose their answers.

Answer Key

1. T 2. F 3. T 4. T

Exercise B.

Have students tell you their answers and write them on the board.

Answer Key

The following things should be checked: sing, dance, meet different families

---

IDEAS FOR . . . **Checking Comprehension**

Ask these additional questions or write them on the board.

1. How did Buck Spotted Tail learn to dance? (He learned from older generations.)
2. Why do you think he says "you try to move like the grass"? What significance does this have? (It could be a way of communicating with nature.)
3. What special meaning does dance have for the Native American people? (It brings people together and celebrates their culture and traditions.)

After Viewing

Discussion

- Tell students to discuss the questions in groups. They can appoint one person as secretary to take notes.
- Ask a spokesperson from each group to present the most interesting ideas to the class.
- Discuss their responses to the photo.

Building Vocabulary
(page 94)

Exercise A. | Meaning from Context

track 2-09

- Tell students to look at the photo, and call on volunteers to describe what is happening.

- Point to Pakistan on a map of the world and ask what students know about it.

- Play the audio while students read.

- Ask some simple comprehension questions. For example: *What is the topic?* (saving energy in Pakistan) *Who is trying to make people save energy? Why?*

Exercise B. | Using a Dictionary

Have students give definitions of any words they know. Then ask them to check their definitions in a dictionary.

Exercise C.

- Tell students to write their answers. Then write the answers on the board.

- Tell students to make their own sentences using these words.

- Discuss any other possible ideas for saving energy.

Answer Key

1. rule 2. customer 3. habit

IDEAS FOR . . . Checking Comprehension

Ask students what they find most surprising about everyday life in Pakistan. For example, that offices do not usually have a two-day weekend, or that people go shopping in the evening.

Using Vocabulary
(page 95)

Exercise A.

- Allow time for students to work individually.

- Check the answers by calling on volunteers to read the sentences aloud.

Answer Key

1. rules 2. shortage 3. lifestyle 4. adapted 5. electricity

Exercise B.

- Allow time for students to work individually.

- Choose two students to read the conversation aloud.

TIP Higher-level students can try to recreate the conversation without looking at their books. Lower-level students can read the conversations again, switching partners. All students can try to continue the interview using information from the reading passage.

Answer Key

1. rules 2. energy 3. electricity 4. shortage 5. Customers 6. adapt 7. lifestyle

Exercise C. | Critical Thinking

- Tell students to work in pairs and make notes of their answers.

- Brainstorm ideas for each question with the whole class.

- Ask students to describe the photo and say what is unusual about it for them.

Developing Listening Skills

45 mins

(pages 96–97)

Pronunciation: The Intonation of *Wh-* Questions

track 2-10

- Remind students that *wh-* questions are *what, when, why, who, where,* and *how.*

- Point out the **Student to Student box**.

- Explain that *wh-* questions produce longer answers than *yes/no* questions and therefore give you more information.

- Play the audio, pausing so that students can repeat.

- You may also want to point out which words have the most stress in these sentences.

- Contrast different ways of answering these questions. For example: *What do customers want?* (They want more electricity./They want air conditioning in the daytime./They want lighting at night time.)

TIP It may be helpful to contrast questions that rise in intonation with questions that rise and then fall. Refer students back to Lesson A page 86 for questions that rise.

Exercise A.

track 2-11

- Play the audio as students draw the intonation patterns.

- Compare the answers as a class.

- Have students practice the conversation in pairs.

> **Answer Key**
>
> A: What are you doing?
>
> A: Why do you look so serious?
>
> B: I can't decide if I want to go to college or stay home and work with my family. What do you think?
>
> A: Hmm, what do your parents say?
>
> A: That's a hard decision. When do you need to decide?

Exercise B.

- Tell students to write the questions.

- Ask them to tell you their answers, and write them on the board.

- Point out that the subject can be replaced by a pronoun in the answer. For example: *When do people shop? They shop in the day.*

> **Answer Key**
>
> 1. Q: When do people shop in Pakistan now?
> 2. Q: Where is there a shortage of electricity?
> 3. Q: Why do banks have a two-day weekend?
> 4. Q: What are people changing?

Exercise C.

Model the intonation and practice the questions as a class before students work in pairs.

Before Listening

- Point to Sweden on a map of the world. Find out what students already know about Sweden.

- Introduce the word *reindeer* and ask what students know about them.

- Read the introduction aloud while students do the exercise.

- Have students tell you their answers and explain why.

- Read the Critical Thinking Focus box.

- Explain that the key words are the lexical items and that they are usually stressed more than the other words. Demonstrate this while reading the paragraph.

> **Answer Key**
>
> 1. T 2. F 3. T 4. F

Vocabulary Note

reindeer (pl. reindeer) is a large deer found in the Arctic regions and in northern America and Europe. Both males and females have large antlers.

Listening: A Short Documentary

Exercise A. | Listening for the Main Idea

track 2-12

- Discuss the meaning of the word *documentary* (a film that is about facts, places, or people)

- Play the audio.

- Discuss the answers as a class.

> **Answer Key**
>
> c. The documentary is about the changing lifestyle of the Sami community.

Exercise B. | Listening for Details

- Remind students of the meanings of *vehicles* and *tradition*.
- Play the audio again.
- Check the answers as a class.

Answer Key

1. animals 2. vehicles 3. changing 4. traditions

After Listening

Critical Thinking

Ask students to think of one example of change that they agree with and one that they disagree with.

> **IDEAS FOR . . . Checking Comprehension**
>
> Tell students to list the positive and negative effects of change on the Sami community.
>
> Discuss possible differences between generations in attitudes towards change in the Sami community.

Exploring Spoken English

(pages 98–99)

30 mins

track 2-13

Exercise A.

- Ask students what they know about Venice. Ask: *Where is Venice?* (in Italy, on the Adriatic Sea) *Why is it famous?* (it has many canals and many beautiful historic buildings) *Why could water be a problem in Venice?* (the sea level is rising) *What is happening in the photo?*
- Play the audio while students read.
- Higher-level students may choose to listen and take notes without reading.

Exercise B. | Discussion

After students have finished discussing the questions, ask them to summarize the information in the passage.

Grammar: Simple Present versus Simple Past Tense of the Verb *To Be*

- Remind students of the two types of questions.
- Ask students to notice the word order in *yes/no* and *wh-* questions. (In *yes/no* questions, the verb comes first.)

- Model the questions giving attention to stress and intonation. Ask students to repeat.
- Remind students of spelling rules for *-ing* forms.

> **IDEAS FOR . . . Presenting Grammar**
>
> Draw a chart on the board and write a few students' names. Ask them to tell you where they were at these different times. Fill in the chart. Then ask them to make sentences about themselves and about each other using the information in the chart and the different forms of the verb *be*.
>
> | | Yesterday | Last week | Last year |
> |---|---|---|---|
> | Peter | | | |
> | Maria | | | |
> | Tony | | | |
> | Krista | | | |
>
> Draw a second chart on the board. Then ask students to tell you where people in their family are right now. Fill in the chart. Then ask them to make sentences about these people using the information in the chart and the different forms of the verb *be*.
>
> | | Right now |
> |---|---|
> | Peter's brother | |
> | Maria's sister | |
> | Tony's parents | |
> | Krista's boyfriend | |
>
> Ask students to make their own charts in pairs.

Exercise A.

Allow time for students to complete their answers individually.

track 2-14

Exercise B.

- Play the audio while students check their answers.
- Write the correct answers on the board.
- You may want to play the audio and have students repeat either as a class or individually.
- Draw students' attention to the stress, rhythm, and intonation and have them try to keep the same speed as the audio.
- Alternatively, students can speak quietly or whisper along with the audio.
- Monitor students and give feedback as they practice in pairs.

Answer Key

1. was 2. are 3. is 4. was 5. was 6. are 7. are 8. are 9. is 10. is

Exercise C. | Discussion

* Monitor students as they work and pick out some good examples of sentences using the past and present forms of the verb *be*.

* Write some of the examples on the board or read them out to the class.

IDEAS FOR . . . Expansion

Ask students to write in their journals about how their home countries have changed. This will help them prepare for the next lesson.

Note: You may want to ask students to bring in a picture of a celebration in their country to use in the next lesson.

Engage: Presenting to a Small Group *(page 100)*

45 mins

WARM-UP

* Bring in pictures of a celebration in your country and show it to the class. Describe how it has changed over the years, perhaps comparing how it was when you were a child and how it is now.

* Read the task. Explain that each student will give their own presentation.

* Brainstorm ideas for different celebrations in your students' countries and write them on the board.

Presentation Skills: Using Graphics

* Read the information in the box.

* Discuss the importance of each point.

Exercise A. | Organizing Ideas

* Model some examples of how you would complete these sentences.

* Allow time for students to work on their presentations. They may want to help each other in pairs or groups.

* Circulate and provide assistance as required.

TIP One way to encourage constructive feedback is to have students ask their partner questions after finishing their presentation. For example, Was my presentation clear? Was my voice loud enough? Was my presentation interesting?

Exercise B. | Practice your Presentation

* Suggest that students stand up and work with a different partner.

* You may want to repeat this step a few times.

Exercise C. | Presentation

* Organize students into small groups and tell each person in the group to take notes on the presentations. They can write the following headings in their notebooks:

Speaking clearly

Using visuals

Using eye contact

Good organization

Interesting information

* Tell each person to present to the others in their group.

* Gather feedback from the class about how they felt about giving their presentations.

IDEAS FOR . . . Expansion

Have students work in pairs or groups to design a questionnaire about how traditions have changed. They can interview someone in the school or a neighbor or family member and present a summary of the information in the next lesson.

Facing Challenges

Academic Pathways

Lesson A: Listening to a Presentation
              Talking about the Past

Lesson B: Listening to a Conversation
              Presenting from Notes

Unit Theme

Unit 6 explores the topic of people who have overcome challenges of different kinds, both physical and environmental.

Think and Discuss *(page 101)*

5 mins

- Point out the unit title and the academic pathways.
- Gather students' interpretations of the unit title.
- Discuss question 1. Ask: *What is special or unusual about the photo? Why do you think this man is climbing a tree? What kind of challenge does the photo show?*
- Discuss question 2. Discuss different areas of science that scientists can study.
- Discuss question 3. Find out what students know about these trees.

Note: A *Sequoia* (pron. si-koi-ya) is a type of redwood coniferous tree found in Northern California and Southern Oregon in the United States. Sequoias are among the largest trees in the world.

Exploring the Theme

15 mins

(pages 102–103)

The opening spread features pictures of several occupations that are challenging and dangerous.

- Discuss various possible meanings of the word *challenging*. For example: *difficult, demanding, dangerous,* but also *testing, stimulating, interesting.*
- Tell students to look at the photos and name the jobs shown there.

- Discuss question 1 as a class. Identify what is dangerous or difficult about the environment shown in each picture.
- Discuss question 2. Brainstorm other jobs that involve working with people or with animals that could be challenging. For example: *teacher, doctor, social worker, zookeeper, veterinarian,* or *animal trainer.* Discuss what motivates people to do these dangerous or difficult jobs.
- Discuss question 3. Rank the jobs shown in order from most to least challenging.
- Ask students to work in groups and list their answers to question 3. Then make a list on the board of the 10 most challenging jobs.
- Discuss question 4 and compare ideas on different ways we can experience challenges in our lives.

Vocabulary Note

A *caiman* is a kind of small alligator found in Central and South America.

IDEAS FOR . . . **Expansion**

Form groups and tell each group to choose a different job. It can be a job from this page or another job. They should discuss what aspects of the job are most challenging and list the positives and negatives of doing that job. Then each group can present the results of their discussion to the class.

Building Vocabulary
(page 104)

WARM-UP

The Lesson A target vocabulary is presented in the context of a professional athlete who is blind.

Ask students to think about a person who inspires or inspired them. *Who is/was he or she? Why or how did they inspire you?*

track 2-15

Exercise A. | Using a Dictionary

- Have students read the vocabulary words and check the ones they already know.
- Play the audio with students repeating each word.
- Correct pronunciation or stress if necessary.
- Give students time to look up any words they're not sure about in the dictionary.

> **TIP** For exercise A, ask which words are easy or difficult to remember. It may be helpful for students to hear each others' tips for remembering the meaning of difficult vocabulary.

Exercise B.

After checking the answers, tell students to make example sentences with each word.

> **Answer Key**
>
> 1. d 2. c 3. b 4. a

Exercise C.

After checking the answers, ask students to give examples of situations in which these things could happen.

> **Answer Key**
>
> 1. challenge 2. inspire 3. climb 4. afraid

track 2-16

Exercise D. | Meaning from Context

- Play the audio as students read.
- Ask questions about any additional vocabulary (besides the words in blue).
- Ask students to identify the seven continents.

Vocabulary Note

vision (= ability to see), let (= allow), athlete (= sportsperson), elementary school (= school for students aged 5 to 10), sighted (= able to see), motivational speaker (= someone who inspires others through their talks).

> **IDEAS FOR . . . Checking Comprehension**
>
> Ask additional questions about the passage or write them on the board.
>
> 1. Which of Erik Weihenmayer's accomplishments do you find most inspiring? Why?
> 2. What questions would you like to ask him if you could meet him?

Using Vocabulary
(page 105)

track 2-17

Exercise A.

- Play the audio while students read.
- Tell students to work individually to write their answers.
- Play the audio again while students check their answers.

> **Answer Key**
>
> 1. climbing 2. professional 3. inspire 4. accomplishments 5. challenges 6. afraid 7. ambition 8. encourage

Exercise B.

Have students practice in pairs. Emphasize using natural intonation and pronunciation.

> **TIP** When students read aloud from the page, their intonation may sound less natural. Advise students first to read the sentence, and then look up as they say the sentence to their partner.

Exercise C. | Discussion

- Have students work in pairs to practice the conversation.
- Ask volunteers to present their conversation to the class.
- Give feedback on pronunciation and intonation.

> **TIP** Higher-level students can try to memorize the conversation. Lower-level students can switch roles and practice the conversation again. Students may continue the conversation with their own ideas.

Developing Listening Skills
(pages 106–107)

45 mins

Before Listening

Predicting Content

- Useful vocabulary: *rock face, steep, climbing gear/ equipment, safety rope*
- Students will check these predictions in exercise **C**.

Listening: A Presentation

track **2-18**

Exercise A. | Listening for Main Ideas

- Tell students to read the statements.
- Play the audio while students choose their answers.
- Compare answers as a class.
- Ask students to explain how they knew the main idea.

Answer Key

2. It is important to be prepared before facing a challenge.

track **2-18**

Exercise B. | Listening for Details

- Have students read the statements.
- Play the audio again. Then have students compare answers with a partner's.

TIP Explain that when we listen we use two different strategies: listening for the main idea and listening for details. We use both strategies at once. Understanding the main idea helps us understand how the details fit together.

Answer Key

The following items should be checked: **1.** Both Erik and Chad are very active. **4.** Erik was hit on the shoulder with a piece of ice while climbing. **5.** Chad uses a special prosthesis to climb.

track **2-18**

Exercise C. | Checking Predictions

Tell students to look back at their predictions and see how many were correct.

Vocabulary Note

prosthesis (= an artificial limb, e.g., hand, foot, arm, leg, made from plastic or carbon fiber, recently also using electronics to convert muscle movements to electric signals).

IDEAS FOR . . . Checking Comprehension

Ask students these additional questions or write them on the board.

1. How did Erik prepare for the climb? (He got as much information as he could about the place. This helped him "see" where he would be climbing.)
2. How did Chad prepare for their climb? (Chad prepared for the climb by practicing with a special prosthesis.)
3. Why do Erik and Chad climb? (Erik enjoys facing challenges and solving problems. Chad likes to stay active and do everything he can to live a happy life. They both want to show the world that they are able to overcome the many different challenges that life presents.)

Note: Bridal Veil Falls is the smallest of the three waterfalls that make up Niagara Falls. It is located on the U.S. side of the falls, in New York State. It is 56 feet (17 meters) wide. The total vertical drop is 181 feet (55 meters).

After Listening

Exercise A. | Making Inferences

Remind students that inferences are conclusions the reader can make about things that are not directly stated.

Answer Key

1. T 2. T 3. T 4. F

Exercise B. | Role-Playing

- Practice saying the question as a class.
- When students have finished, ask them to tell you their ideas for questions 2 and 3 and write them on the board.

TIP You may want to use exercise B to lead into a broader discussion of the challenges of being a student and what tips and solutions students have found to deal with them. This can give you useful information about how to help students.

Answer Key

Answers will vary.

Exercise C. | Self-Reflection

Call on volunteers to share their answers.

Pronunciation: The Simple Past Tense *-ed* Endings

track 2-19

You may want to contrast the /d/ sound with the other two sounds of *-ed* (/t/ and /id/). These sounds will be taught in Lesson **B** on page 116 of this unit.

track 2-20

Play the audio and pause after each word. Students can repeat as a class or individually.

> TIP
> You may want to point out that the *-ed* sound often gets linked with the next word in a sentence, which can sometimes make it difficult to hear. For example: *He listened to music.*

Exploring Spoken English

45 mins

(pages 108–109)

Language Function: Expressing Difficulty with Something

- Brainstorm some things people often have difficulty with. For example, being on time or remembering names. Make a list on the board.
- Ask students to make similar sentences about themselves using the expressions in the box.
- Point out that *have a hard time* is more informal (conversational/spoken) than the other expressions.

> **IDEAS FOR . . . Expansion**
>
> Have students write down one thing they are good at and one thing they find challenging. Then have them stand up and walk around the class. They should ask questions to find out how many students share the same challenges as they do, and how many people are good at the things they themselves find difficult.

Exercise A.

- Pair students to compare their answers.
- Ask if students know anything more about these famous people or if they know of any other famous people who had a hard time getting started but later became very successful.

> **Answer Key**
>
> **1.** had a hard time **2.** was challenging **3.** was difficult

Exercise B.

- Give students time to complete the exercise.
- Form groups. Have students compare their answers.

- Choose a spokesperson from each group to tell the class the most interesting answers.
- Find out if there is anything that all groups have in common.

> **Answer Key**
>
> Answers will vary.

Exercise C. | Collaboration

Useful vocabulary: *rickshaws, traffic jam, heat, dust, noise, pollution.*

> **Answer Key**
>
> Answers will vary.

Grammar: Irregular Past Tense Verbs

You may want to introduce this section with a quiz on past tense forms to see what students already know.

> **IDEAS FOR . . . Presenting Grammar**
>
> Tell each student to write down one interesting thing that they did last week on a slip of paper. Collect the papers and mix them up. Hand them out again at random.
>
> Students have to walk around the classroom and ask questions to find the person who wrote the sentence on the paper they have. For example: *Did you see a movie last week?* When they find the person, they should ask three additional questions about the event and write down the answers.
>
> When students have finished, ask each student to tell the class about the information they found out.

Exercise A.

After checking the answers, ask students to make one or two additional sentences using these verbs.

> **Answer Key**
>
> **1.** Did **2.** was **3.** went **4.** gave

Exercise B. | Group Discussion

Student to Student: Taking Turns

Explain that it is important to participate in a group discussion, but it is also important not to take over and prevent others from speaking. Using these phrases will help ensure that all group members have a chance to participate equally.

Exercise C.

Monitor students as they work to see if they have any difficulties using the irregular past tense forms or the expressions for taking turns.

Answer Key

Wording of answers will vary.

1. Yes, it was difficult for J.K. Rowling to get her book published.
2. No, the challenge of getting her first book published did not stop her from writing more books.
3. Yes, Soichiro Honda had a hard time finding a job as an engineer.
4. Yes, he became a successful businessperson.

Exploring Spoken English

(page 110)

Exercise D.

track 2-21

- Tell students to look at the photo and ask if anyone can name this musical instrument (xylophone). *Has anyone played one? How does it work?* (by hitting wooden bars with a mallet; each bar is tuned to a different musical pitch).
- Ask what other musical instruments work by hitting something to make a sound. (For example: drum, cymbals, gong, piano.)
- Ask students to suggest how a deaf person might be able to sense music.
- Compile a list of the past tense verbs on the board. Ask for the base form of each one.

Answer Key

Evelyn Glennie is a famous percussionist and composer. Like every musician, Evelyn has a challenging job. As a young musician, she spent hours and hours practicing and learning different musical instruments. And because she wanted to be a composer as well, she spent even more hours learning music theory and practicing songwriting. However, Evelyn is a little different from other musicians. She is deaf. She lost most of her hearing when she was 12 years old. But that didn't stop her from becoming a musician. Evelyn knew she had a special connection to her music. She learned how to listen to music by letting sound waves travel through her body. Evelyn's music is so beautiful that she was invited to play at the opening ceremony of the 2012 Olympics. Evelyn did not let being deaf stop her from doing what she wanted to do. Even though she has a hard job, she is successful at it. She is an inspiration to musicians around the world and to all of us.

Exercise E.

Ask students what they find most interesting about Evelyn Glennie.

Answer Key

Wording of answers will vary.
1. She was 12 when she lost her hearing.
2. She learned to play different instruments by practicing for hours.
3. She studied music theory and songwriting.
4. No, Evelyn listens to music through her body.
5. Evelyn's job is challenging because she is deaf.

Exercise F. | Group Discussion

Ask students to discuss how these people could inspire others.

Speaking *(page 111)*

30-45 mins

Talking about the Past

Exercise A.

track 2-22

- Review the words in the box and practice the pronunciation if necessary.
- Play the audio while students read.
- Practice the pronunciation of any difficult names or words, such as Alistair Humphreys, M25, Thames.
- Have students point out the past tense verbs.

Answer Key

1. professional 2. inspire 3. challenges 4. encourages
5. afraid 6. ambition

Exercise B.

- Encourage students to ask additional questions in order to get more detailed information from their partner.
- You may want to announce when partners should switch roles.

Answer Key

Wording of answers will vary.
1. Yes, he likes challenges.
2. He walked along the M25, he swam the Thames, he slept outside, and he lived off the land for four days.
3. He made videos to inspire people.
4. He learned that people can be successful no matter how hard the challenges are.

Exercise C. | Group Discussion

Tell students to think of reasons and details to support their arguments.

Exercise D. | Self-Reflection

Call on students to tell the class about their partner's experience.

Viewing: Antarctic Challenge *(pages 112–113)*

30 mins

Overview of the Video

The video is about a team of climbers who climbed a very tall rock in Antarctica.

WARM-UP

Point to Antarctica on a map or globe and ask students what they know about it. What is the South Pole?

Note: *Antarctica* is the earth's most southernmost continent. It contains the South Pole. (The South Pole is the southern point of the earth where the earth's axis of rotation intersects its surface.)

Before Viewing

Exercise A. | Critical Thinking

Pair students to answer the questions. They may want to list their answers in a chart.

Difficulties of getting to Antarctica	What or who lives there?	Difficulties of living there

Answer Key

Answers will vary.

Exercise B.
track 2-23

Ask students if they would like to visit Antarctica. Why, or why not?

> **TIP** To make this more challenging, ask higher level students to listen with their books closed and take notes while they listen. Then use their notes to answer the questions in exercise C.

Exercise C.

After students have compared answers in pairs, check the answers as a class and write them on the board.

Answer Key

Wording of answers will vary.
1. Antarctica covers over 5 million square miles.
2. Summer in Antarctica is between November and February.
3. Tourists can see frozen land, icebergs, whales, seals, and penguins in Antarctica.

While Viewing

Exercise A.

Give students time to read all the questions before watching.

Answer Key

1. plane **2.** rock **3.** snow **4.** fall

Exercise B.

Play the video again while students write their answers.

Answer Key

The following items should be checked: plane, snowmobile.

Exercise C.

- Give students time to read the statements before playing the video.
- Ask students to correct the false statements.

Answer Key

1. T **2.** T **3.** F **4.** F

IDEAS FOR . . . Checking Comprehension

Ask these additional questions.

1. What kind of weather did they have? (It was cold and windy.)
2. Why was it difficult to climb the rock? (There was no place to put their hands or feet, and they had to feel their way up. The rock was very sharp and made their hands bleed.)
3. What kind of equipment and supplies do you think they had to take with them? (Answers will vary.)

After Viewing

Discussion

Have one partner present the most interesting ideas to the class.

Building Vocabulary
30 mins
(page 114)

track 2-24
Exercise A. | Using a Dictionary

- Ask which words they know and in which contexts they have come across them.
- Play the audio and pause after each word for students to repeat.
- Give students time to look up any words they aren't sure of.

Exercise B.

- Give students time to write their answers.
- Check the answers by having students say sentences and give examples when appropriate. For example: *An activity is something that you spend time doing. For example, mountain climbing.*

Answer Key

1. obstacle 2. realize 3. sled 4. environment 5. goal
6. activity 7. equipment

track 2-25
Exercise C.

- Point out the photo. Ask: *Where are they and what are they doing? What is the landscape like?*
- Point out that the instructions call for the correct *form* of the word that will fit the gap. (Item 1 is the past tense form, for example, and item 7 is the plural form.)
- Play the audio while students write their answers.
- More advanced students may opt to write their answers first, and then check them by playing the audio.

Answer Key

1. realized 2. goal 3. sled 4. environment 5. obstacles
6. equipment 7. activities

Note: The **Iditarod Trail Sled Dog Race** is an annual sled dog race run in Alaska. The sleds are pulled by teams of 12 to 16 dogs and cover the distance in 9 to 15 days. The teams often have to race through snow blizzards, sub-zero temperatures, and gale-force winds.

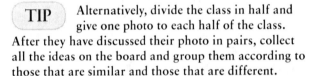

IDEAS FOR . . . Checking Comprehension

Ask these additional questions about inferences that can be made from the reading and have students discuss them in pairs.

1. What personal qualities does Dr. Davis need in his job?
2. Why does he love his job?

Using Vocabulary
(page 115)

Exercise A. | Discussion

- Ask students to describe the environments in the photos.
- Ask: *What is similar about these two environments, and what is different?*
- Have students work in pairs to make a list of challenges posed by these environments.

TIP Alternatively, divide the class in half and give one photo to each half of the class. After they have discussed their photo in pairs, collect all the ideas on the board and group them according to those that are similar and those that are different.

track 2-26
Exercise B.

- Allow time for students to work individually.
- Play the audio as students check their answers.

Answer Key

1. goal 2. environment 3. realized 4. activities
5. equipment 6. obstacles

Exercise C. | Role-Playing

- Pair students to practice the conversation.
- Monitor students as they work and give feedback on intonation and pronunciation.

Exercise D. | Critical Thinking

- Brainstorm different types of work environments.
- Ask each group to choose one type of environment and discuss its challenges.

Developing Listening Skills

45 mins

(pages 116–117)

track 2-27

Pronunciation: The Simple Past Tense *-ed* Endings

- Remind students about the /d/ sound they studied in Lesson **A** on page 107.
- Introduce these two additional sounds and play the audio so that students can listen to the difference.

> **TIP** It may be helpful to label each sound with a number. /t/ is sound number 1, and /id/ is sound number 2. Then students can identify whether they hear sound 1 or sound 2.

track 2-28

Exercise A.

Play the audio and pause so that students can repeat (individually or as a class).

track 2-29

Exercise B.

- Explain that students will hear a word and they will have to decide which sound they hear.
- Play the audio while students circle their answers.

Answer Key

1. /t/ 2. /id/ 3. /t/ 4. /id/ 5. /t/

Exercise C.

- Allow time for students to complete their charts.
- Draw the chart on the board.
- Choose individual students to come to the board and write one word in the correct place in the chart.
- Ask the class if they agree and then repeat the word as a class.
- As a follow-up, have students work in pairs. Student A says the verb in the past tense. Student B says which sound it is (without looking at the chart).

Answer Key

/**t**/ watched, worked, liked, talked, jumped; /**d**/ loved, wished, faced, played, listened, inspired, enjoyed, climbed, watched; /**id**/ wanted, added, hunted

Before Listening

Prior Knowledge

- Point out the photos. Find out what students know about a taxi driver's job and a chef's job.
- While students discuss the questions in pairs, walk around the class and write down the most interesting ideas.
- Call on pairs with the most interesting ideas to explain their answers to the class.

Answer Key

Answers will vary.

Listening: A Conversation

track 2-30

Exercise A. | Listening for the Main Idea

Discuss the answers as a class.

Answer Key

b. the challenges of their work

track 2-30

Exercise B. | Listening for Details

- Allow time for students to read the conversations and complete as much as they can remember.
- Play the audio again.
- Check the answers as a class.

Answer Key

1. taxi driver; chef 2. New York 3. a) 10 b) nice
4. a) worked b) Customers

After Listening

Self-Reflection

You may want to ask students to take roles, so that Student A argues that the chef's job is better and Student B argues that the taxi driver's job is better.

> **IDEAS FOR . . . Checking Comprehension**
>
> Play the audio again and ask students to add any extra details about each person's life or job. For example, *The taxi driver didn't have much time to see his family or friends. If the chef made a small mistake with an order, his customers and supervisor complained.*

Exploring Spoken English
(pages 118–119)

Exercise A. | Making Inferences
track 2-31

- Go over the Critical Thinking Focus box.
- Discuss why it is important to be able to make inferences. (Not all of the meaning is contained in the words of the text; the reader also has to draw his or her own conclusions.)
- Play the audio while students read.
- Call on individual students to explain their answers.

Answer Key

1. c 2. a 3. b

TIP To make exercise A more challenging, you may want to write the sentences on the board and ask students to make inferences without looking at the choices.

Exercise B.
track 2-32

- Explain that students will listen to a conversation.
- Play the audio and ask students for the main idea.
- Play the audio again as students choose their answers.

Answer Key

1. b 2. c 3. a 4. b

Exercise C. | Discussion

After students have discussed the questions, you may want to lead into a broader discussion of whether men and women need different qualities in order to succeed in business and why there are fewer successful businesswomen than men and how they would go about changing this.

Grammar: The Simple Past Tense

- Remind students of regular and irregular simple past tense forms.
- Go over the information and examples in the box.
- Point out that past tense time expressions can refer to a point of time (*yesterday, last week, two days ago*) or a period of time (*for a month, for three weeks*).
- Discuss as a class other past tense time expressions.

IDEAS FOR . . . Presenting Grammar

Students can work in groups to make a quiz about famous explorers or pioneers or people who faced significant challenges in their lives. The quiz should list 10 names and 10 things that these people did in mixed-up order. Groups can exchange their quizzes and try to match up the names with the actions.

Examples: Roald Amundsen, Neil Armstrong, Edmund Hillary, Nelson Mandela, Helen Keller, Amelia Earhart.

While students are working, move around the class and provide help with vocabulary.

At the end of the activity, list the verbs on the board and check that everyone understands the meaning and can form the past tense correctly.

Exercise A.
track 2-33

- Allow time for students to complete their answers individually.
- Play the audio so that students can check their answers.
- Ask volunteers to read out their sentences.

Answer Key

1. started 2. makes 3. walked 4. practice 5. is

Answer Key

1. a 2. b 3. a 4. b

Exercise B.

- Allow time for students to complete their answers individually.
- Ask volunteers to read out their sentences.

Exercise C. | Critical Thinking

- Ask students to describe in some detail what each person in the photos does in his or her job.
- You may want to ask students to complete a chart or a diagram with their answers.

Answer Key

Answers will vary.

Engage: Presenting from Notes *(page 120)*

45 mins

Note: You will need to bring in some index cards for students to use for this lesson, or pieces of paper of approximately the same size as index cards (about four to six cards per student).

WARM-UP

- Prepare a short two-minute talk about a challenge that you have faced in your life.
- Make notes for your talk on index cards.
- Tell the class about your challenge.
- Ask students to notice *how* you are giving the talk and to take notes of any tips that could help them.
- While you are speaking, make sure to glance at your notes but then look at the class while you are speaking. Make sure to make eye contact and to pause frequently.
- When you are finished, ask students to tell you any points they noticed about how you gave the talk. You may also ask them to give you tips for improvement.

  For example:

  You made notes on index cards.

  You looked at the cards but didn't read them.

  You made eye contact.

  You paused frequently.

  You spoke clearly and slowly.

Presentation Skills: Presenting to a Group Using Notes

- Present the information in the box.
- Discuss the importance of using notes.
- Ask individuals to read out each bulleted item.
- Discuss why you shouldn't read from the notes. (Because you will be looking down and your voice will not be easy to hear. Also, your voice will not sound as natural or as interesting if you are reading instead of speaking.)
- Give some examples from your notes to illustrate what the notes should look like.

Exercise A. | Self-Reflection

- Brainstorm some ideas with the whole class for different types of challenges at school, in sports, or at work.
- Allow time for each student to choose one idea for his or her talk.
- If students are stuck for ideas, suggest they write down as many ideas as they can and then choose the best one.

Exercise B. | Organizing Ideas

- Explain the importance of breaking down the presentation into stages or steps.
- Advise students to add as much detail as possible to each step by asking themselves questions: *Why was it difficult? What inspired them to overcome this challenge? What was their goal? What helped them the most?*
- Write vocabulary words from this unit on the board and encourage students to use them in their presentations: *accomplishment, inspire, afraid, ambition, obstacle, goal, realize, encourage.*

Exercise C. | Making Notes

Explain that notes for each step of the presentation will go on a separate index card.

Exercise D. | Presentation

- Form groups of five or six students.
- Each member of the group will do their presentation for the group.
- Remind the other members of the group to give feedback on the presentation, especially on how they used their notes.

IDEAS FOR . . . Expansion

Ask students to do some research about a famous explorer, pioneer, or someone who overcame challenges in the past. What inspired them? What obstacles did they have to overcome? How did they manage to overcome those obstacles?

Students should prepare notes on index cards and give a presentation about their chosen person (to the class or in small groups) in the next lesson.

Lost and Found

Academic Pathways

Lesson A: Listening to a Guided Tour
              Talking about the Past

Lesson B: Listening to a Conversation
              Role-Playing

Unit Theme

Unit 7 explores the topic of ancient civilizations that have disappeared and that we now study through archaeology.

5 mins

Think and Discuss *(page 121)*

- Point out the unit title and the academic pathways.

- Ask students how they think the title might relate to the photo.

- Discuss question 1. Useful vocabulary: *mask, gold, decorated, inlaid, striped, ornamental, buried, mummy.*

- Discuss question 2. Ask students what they know about Ancient Egypt and its culture.

- Discuss question 3. Ask students to brainstorm ideas about any lost ancient cultures.

Note: Tutankhamun (pron. too-TANK-ah-MOON) was an Egyptian pharaoh who ruled from around 1332 BC to 1323 BC. His tomb, including this magnificent burial mask, was discovered intact by archaeologists in 1922.

15 mins

Exploring the Theme
(pages 122–123)

The opening spread features a timeline of various ancient civilizations with photos of artifacts belonging to each civilization.

- Discuss the ancient civilizations shown on this page. Ask: *Which is the oldest? Which was the most recent? How many years ago did each civilization exist? Which continents were they on? What do students know about each one? What do you think these artifacts were used for? What other ancient civilizations do you know of?*

- Discuss what makes a civilization, what causes it to flourish (grow) and what can cause it to disappear. Ask students to give examples to support their opinions.

- Discuss questions 1 and 2 as a class. Why is archaeology important? What kind of artifacts have archaeologists found? What do they tell us about the past?

- Discuss question 3. You may want to limit the discussion to the four civilizations shown here, or include any others that students are familiar with.

Note: BC (before Christ), AD (anno Domini = in the year of our Lord)

IDEAS FOR ... Expansion

Divide the class into four groups. Assign one of these civilizations to each group. Tell them to research some interesting and surprising facts about each civilization and tell the class in the next lesson.

30 mins

Building Vocabulary
(page 124)

WARM-UP

The Lesson A target vocabulary is presented in the context of the ancient Cambodian kingdom of Angkor Wat.

▪ Find out what students know about Cambodia or Angkor Wat.

▪ Ask if they can guess any reasons why this kingdom disappeared.

Exercise A. | Using a Dictionary

track 2-34

▪ Play the audio and have students repeat each word (optional).

▪ Correct pronunciation or stress if necessary.

Exercise B.

After checking the answers, tell students to make example sentences with each word.

Answer Key

1. b 2. d 3. a 4. c

Exercise C. | Meaning from Context

track 2-35

▪ Ask students to describe the photo. What kind of landscape is shown? What manmade features are in the photo?

▪ Play the audio as students read.

▪ Ask questions about any additional vocabulary (not the words in blue).

Vocabulary Note

kingdom (= country ruled by king or queen), royal (= connected with kings or queens), teachings (= philosophy, system of ideas), waterway (= canal for water)

Answer Key

1. resources 2. temples 3. century 4. valuable

IDEAS FOR . . . **Checking Comprehension**

Ask additional questions about the passage or write them on the board.

1. Name four unusual things about Angkor Wat.
2. Name four possible reasons for its disappearance.

30 mins

Using Vocabulary
(page 125)

Exercise A.

Tell students to work individually to write their answers.

Answer Key

1. century 2. capital 3. emperors 4. temples
5. valuable 6. Internal

Exercise B.

track 2-36

▪ Play the audio while students check their answers.

▪ Pair students to practice the conversation.

▪ Emphasize using natural intonation and pronunciation.

TIP Students may want to try making their own similar conversations based on information in the reading.

Exercise C. | Discussion

▪ Ask students to describe the photo. What is unusual about it?

▪ Allow time for students to work in pairs. Then gather their ideas as a class.

▪ For question 2, you may want to discuss which countries had emperors in the past. For example: India, China, Persia.

Vocabulary Note

moat (= a canal or ditch filled with water that surrounds a palace or a castle)

45 mins

Developing Listening Skills
(pages 126–127)

Before Listening

Prior Knowledge

Have students work in groups and brainstorm as many ideas as they can concerning the purposes of a museum and the possible uses of the object in this photo.

Note: The British Museum is a museum in London dedicated to human history and culture. It has one of the largest collections of human artifacts and illustrates the development of human civilizations from all continents from its origins to the present day. It used to house the British Library, but this has now moved to another location.

Listening: A Guided Tour

track **2-37**

Exercise A. | Listening for Main Ideas

- Ask students to describe the photo and suggest what it might be.
- Allow time for students to read the statements.
- Play the audio while students choose their answers.
- Compare answers as a class.

> **Answer Key**
>
> **1.** b **2.** a **3.** c

track **2-37**

Exercise B. | Listening for Details

- Tell students to read the statements.
- Play the audio again. Then have students compare their answers in pairs.
- Play difficult sections of the audio again, if necessary, to clarify any answers.
- Ask students what part of the British Museum they would most like to visit.

> **Answer Key**
>
> **1.** b **2.** c **3.** a **4.** c

IDEAS FOR . . . Checking Comprehension

Ask students these additional questions or write them on the board.

1. Where is the British Museum? (in London)
2. When was it first opened to the public? (in 1753)
3. What is in the center? (the Round Reading Room)
4. Where can you see a copy of the Cyrus Cylinder? (the United Nations in New York City)

After Listening

Exercise A. | Self-Reflection

- Ask students to describe the photo. What are these people doing?
- Did any students go on museum visits when they were in high school? Did they enjoy them? Why or why not?
- Encourage students to support their answers with examples of museums they have visited. They may want to compare different kinds of museums and say why they find some more interesting than others.

Exercise B. | Critical Thinking

Encourage students to think of as many possible answers as they can.

Pronunciation: Word Stress

track **2-38**

- Introduce the information about word stress.
- Play the audio and pause so that students can repeat.

> **TIP** You may want to review the meaning of the word *syllable* and ask students to identify the number of syllables in words such as *emperor, century, museum, civilization,* or other words from this lesson.

track **2-39**

Exercise A.

- Play the audio and pause after each word so that students can underline the correct syllable.
- Alternatively, ask students to underline the syllables first and then play the audio to check their answers.
- Play the audio again so that students can repeat the words.

> **Answer Key**
>
> **1.** temple **2.** paper **3.** answer **4.** people **5.** prevent
> **6.** survive **7.** quiet **8.** explain **9.** sleepy **10.** perfect

> **TIP** When asking students to repeat as a class, you can ask them to whisper or murmur the word quietly. This can help to avoid exaggerated stress or intonation.

Exercise B.

As you listen, identify which words students have trouble with and practice those again as a class.

45 mins

Exploring Spoken English
(pages 128–129)

Grammar: Informational Past Tense Questions

- You may want to introduce this section by writing two *yes/no* questions on the board, one with the past tense of *be* and one with the past tense of another verb. For example: *Were you at school yesterday? Did you go to the library yesterday?*

- Ask students to identify differences in form between these two questions. (For example: *In the first example, there is only one verb. In the second example, the verb has two parts.*)

- Then introduce the information in the box.

Exercise A.

Check the answers before students practice the conversation with their partner.

Answer Key

1. Were 2. Were 3. build 4. Was 5. Were

Exercise B.

Check the answers as a class. Then tell students to use the questions to make a conversation.

Answer Key

1. <u>Did</u> you <u>see</u> your friend yesterday?
2. <u>Did</u> the boy <u>visit</u> Pompeii last summer?
3. <u>Did</u> Claire <u>take</u> pictures of the Cyrus Cylinder last month?
4. <u>Did</u> the family <u>think</u> Angkor Wat was interesting?

Language Function: Expressing Past Facts and Generalizations with *Used To*

- Introduce the information in the box.

- Practice the pronunciation of *used to.* You may want to distinguish this from the pronunciation of the verb *use*, for example, *Sand is used to /juːztu/ make glass.*

- You may also want to teach question forms with *used to* as they will come up in exercises **B** and **F** in this lesson.

IDEAS FOR . . . Expansion

Draw a chart on the board with two columns for *past* and *now*. In the first column, write three things you used to do that you don't do now and in the second column three things that you do now instead. For example, Past: play soccer; Now: go cycling.

Then ask students to do the same for themselves and tell their partner. Then ask volunteers to tell you about their partner's information. Find out how many had the same or similar sentences.

Exercise A.

Check the answers by calling on individuals to read out their sentences.

Answer Key

1. used to treat 2. used to build 3. used to have 4. used to rule

Exercise B.

- Ask students to describe the picture.

- Have partners make up three more questions about the picture using *used to.*

Answer Key

1. Yes, people in ancient Greece used to build walls around the cities.
2. Yes, men used to wear short dresses.
3. Yes, women used to wear long, colorful dresses.
4. Yes, people in ancient Greece used to travel on horses.

Exercise C.

To add an extra challenge, ask students to cover the right hand column and make up their own ending for each sentence.

Answer Key

1. d 2. c 3. a 4. b

Exercise D. | Making Inferences

Encourage students to come up with as many answers as possible.

Exploring Spoken English
(page 130)

track 2-40

Exercise E.

- Ask students to look at the photo and suggest what this object might have been used for.
- Find out what students know about Aztec, Olmec, and Maya civilizations. (Refer back to page 123 for information about the Maya civilization.)
- Play the audio while students read the passage.
- Allow students time to read silently and underline verbs.
- Ask students which information they found most surprising and why.

Answer Key

Three thousand years ago, ancient civilizations in Mexico and Central America <u>used to</u> make rubber. The Aztec, Olmec, and Maya civilizations <u>used to</u> make rubber from trees and plants. Some of the rubber they made <u>used to</u> bounce. The Mayas <u>used to</u> play a lot of ball games. They made balls for their games with this rubber. In ancient Maya, games <u>used to</u> play an important part in their religion. These ball games were played to show good against evil. Sometimes the games ended in human sacrifice. The losers were beheaded—that means they <u>used to</u> have their heads cut off!

Exercise F.

Students who want an extra challenge can cover up the article and try to answer from memory.

Answer Key

Answers will vary. Possible answers include:

1. They used to make rubber.
2. They used to make rubber from trees and plants.
3. Yes, the rubber used to bounce.
4. Yes, they used to play ball games.
5. They used to play ball games to show good against evil.
6. They used to be beheaded.

Exercise G. | Critical Thinking

Ask if students know *ulama* or any other unusual or traditional ball games.

Speaking *(page 131)*

30-45 mins

Talking about the Past

Exercise A.

- Discuss the pictures as a class and ask what students know about each civilization. *Where was each one located geographically? What is shown in each picture? Is it a photo or an illustration?*
- Discuss the timeline and how it shows the relative age of each civilization. *Where would they place the year 1 on this timeline?*

Answer Key

1. No. The Maya civilization came after the Roman Empire.
2. No. The Persian Empire came before the Inca civilization.
3. Yes. The Roman Empire came before the Inca civilization.
4. Yes. The Inca civilization came after the Roman Empire.

Exercise B.

- Brainstorm ideas about what the civilizations from exercise **A** might have in common, and write the ideas on the board.
- Check the answers by asking students to answer the questions with books closed.
- Refer to the list on the board to check predictions.

Answer Key

1. Ancient civilizations had six different characteristics. Answers will vary but should include any three of the following: 1. They lived in big areas. 2. They made large monuments. 3. They had a written language. 4. They had a system for controlling people and land. 5. The people did different types of work. 6. They had social classes.

2. monument

3. Monuments often had unique art on them.

Exercise C. | Self-Reflection

Tell students to support their opinions with examples.

> ### IDEAS FOR . . . Expansion
>
> Ask students to research one ancient civilization and tell the class about it. It can be one on this page or a different one. Find out whether it has each of the characteristics mentioned in the passage in exercise **B**.

30 mins

Viewing: The Lost World of Angkor *(pages 132–133)*

Overview of the Video

The video is about the lost city of Angkor Wat, which used to be the capital of the Khmer Empire in present day Cambodia.

WARM-UP

Point to Cambodia on a map or globe and ask students what they know about it and about the surrounding countries. What do they know about its history, its geography, its language, its people, its culture? Refer students back to the information about Angkor Wat on page 124.

Before Viewing

Exercise A. | Understanding Visuals

- Ask what the map shows.
- Then tell students to discuss the questions.
- Discuss the answers as a class.

Answer Key

1. Rice fields 2. Yes.

Exercise B. | Prior Knowledge

Tell students to refer back to page 124 if necessary.

Exercise C. | Using a Dictionary

- Ask students which words they already know and if they can make example sentences with those words.
- Ask students to find the meanings in the dictionary. What other meanings do these words have?

Answer Key

1. b 2. d 3. a 4. c

While Viewing

Exercise A. | Viewing for Numbers

- Give students time to read all the sentences before watching.
- Play the video while students write their answers.
- Choose volunteers to come to the board and write their answers.

Answer Key

1. 500; 600 2. 1860 3. 200 4. 12th

Exercise B.

- Give students time to read all the sentences before watching.
- Play the video again while students write their answers.
- Compare answers as a class and write them on the board.

Answer Key

1. F 2. T 3. T 4. T

After Viewing

Exercise A. | Critical Thinking

- Ask students to discuss the questions in groups. They can choose one person to be scribe to take notes.
- Ask a spokesperson from each group to present the most interesting ideas to the class.

Exercise B. | Discussion

Encourage students to ask each other questions about the photo.

Building Vocabulary
(page 134)

track 2-41

Exercise A. | Using a Dictionary

- Play the audio and pause after each word for students to repeat.
- Ask students to identify the word stress in multisyllabic words.

Exercise B.

- Check the answers by asking one student to read a word and a different student to read out the definition.
- Write the answers on the board.

Answer Key

1. native 2. artifact 3. chief 4. treasures 5. excavate 6. site 7. gold 8. estimate

track 2-42

Exercise C. | Meaning from Context

- Ask students to describe the photo.
- Ask them to read the title and guess what this artifact could be.
- Point to the country of Panama on a globe or a map.
- Ask what students know about Panama.
- Play the audio while students read.
- Answer any questions about vocabulary that is not in blue.

Vocabulary Note

warrior (= soldier or fighter), cultured (= interested in art and music)

> **IDEAS FOR . . . Checking Comprehension**
>
> Tell students to summarize the main ideas in the passage in two or three sentences.

Using Vocabulary
(page 135)

Exercise A.

- Allow time for students to work individually to complete their answers.
- Check the answers by asking volunteers to read out sentences.

Answer Key

1. site 2. artifacts/treasures 3. chief 4. gold 5. native 6. excavate 7. estimates

Exercise B. | Discussion

- Ask students to describe the photo. Ask: *What are they doing? What tools are they using? What skills do they need?*
- Then have students work in pairs to discuss the questions.

Exercise C. | Self-Reflection

- Pair students to discuss the questions.
- Ask anyone who has worked on an archaeological site, or has knowledge about one, to describe it for the others.
- Discuss why this kind of work is important.

> **IDEAS FOR . . . Expansion**
>
> Students can role-play an interview with archaeologist Julia Mayo using the information from the passage in exercise **C** on page 134. First, ask pairs to make a list of 10 questions. Then have them switch with another partner and role-play the interview. Then they can switch roles and do the interview again. Remind them to use the new vocabulary from this lesson.

Developing Listening Skills
(pages 136–137)

45 mins

Listening for Emphasized Words
track 2-43

- Write a sentence on the board and say the sentence, carefully emphasizing one or two words. For example: Did you **find** any **gold**?

- Ask students to identify which words were louder or stronger.

- Explain that the most important words (words that carry the most meaning) are usually stressed more than the other words (grammatical words).

- Point out that word stress often depends on the intention of the speaker (which point they want to draw attention to).

- Go over the information in the box and play the audio.

- Have students repeat the examples.

> **TIP** It may be helpful to hum the stress pattern or use nonsense syllables like dee-dee-DEE-dee-dee-DEE to illustrate the stress pattern.

Before Listening

Exercise A.
track 2-44

- Allow time for students to read all the sentences.

- Play the audio while students choose their answers.

- Compare answers as a class.

- Alternatively, ask students to predict which words will be stressed and then listen to check if they were right.

- You may want to ask students to repeat the sentences using the same stress pattern.

Answer Key

1. a 2. c 3. c 4. c 5. c

Exercise B. | Predicting Content

- Allow time for students to read all the sentences.

- Emphasize that there are no correct answers at this stage. They will check their predictions after listening to the audio.

Answer Key

Answers will vary.

Listening: A Conversation

Exercise A. | Listening for Details
track 2-45

- Allow time for students to read all the sentences.

- Play the audio.

- Compare answers as a class.

Answer Key

1. c 2. a 3. c

Exercise B. | Note-Taking
track 2-45

- Allow time for students to read the conversation and complete as much as they can remember.

- Play the audio again.

- Check the answers as a class.

Answer Key

1. treasure 2. gold 3. estimate 4. artifacts 5. 120
6. 2,000 7. excavate 8. site

Exercise C. | Checking Predictions
track 2-45

- Refer students back to their answers in exercise **B** on the previous page.

- Play the audio again if necessary.

After Listening

Critical Thinking

- Tell students to look at the photo. Discuss the differences between this photo and the one on page 135.

- Tell each group to come up with at least five different options.

- Write them all on the board.

- Take a class vote on which one they would choose.

Exploring Spoken English
(pages 138–139)

30 mins

Grammar: The Conjunction *Because*

- Present the information in the box.
- Explain that *because* introduces information that answers the question *why?*
- You may want to mention that *because* can also come at the beginning of a sentence, but in this case the first clause is followed by a comma.

> **IDEAS FOR ... Presenting Grammar**
>
> Ask students to work in pairs. Student A will describe what they did in their last vacation, or last weekend. Student B will interrupt as often as possible using questions with *Why?*
>
> For example:
> A: I went to Spain.
> B: Why did you go to Spain?
> A: Because I wanted to practice my Spanish.

track 2-46

Exercise A. | Using a Dictionary

- Tell students to look at the photo. Ask: *What is it? What do you think caused the holes?*
- Play the audio while students read.
- Ask them to underline any new words and use their dictionary to find the meanings.
- Discuss the meanings of the new words.
- Encourage students to use the context to figure out the exact meaning.

Vocabulary Note

skull (= bony part of head, shown in picture),
surgeon (= doctor who operates on the human body),
natives (= people who originally come from a place),
patient (= person who is sick), procedure (= surgical operation), injured (= hurt), surgery (= operation), severe (= serious), trauma (= shock or injury)

Exercise B.

After students have discussed their answers in pairs, choose volunteers to write their answers on the board.

> **Answer Key**
>
> Answers will vary. Possible answers include:
>
> 1. They showed how Inca surgeons used to treat head injuries.
> 2. They had head injuries.
> 3. The procedure was new.

Exercise C.

Discuss the answers as a class. Gather as many answers as possible.

> **Answer Key**
>
> Answers will vary. Possible answers include:
>
> 1. The men probably needed head surgery because they were injured while fighting.
> 2. Ninety percent of the men survived the procedure by the 1400s because the surgeons had more experience.
> 3. Surgeons perform similar procedures today on people who have severe head trauma.

Student to Student: Asking for Clarification

- Ask students what they usually say when they don't understand something.
- Write all their suggestions on the board.
- Review the information in the box.
- Practice these expressions using correct stress and intonation.
- Demonstrate using these expressions by saying something indistinctly so that students have to ask you for clarification.

track 2-47

Exercise D.

- Play the audio while students read.
- Ask students to identify the clarification expressions.
- Ask them to explain what a spa city is and what a bathhouse is.
- Ask students to describe the photo and say how it is similar to or different from a normal bathroom in a house.

> **Answer Key**
>
> A: Last summer we went to Turkey. We visited an ancient Roman spa city!
> B: I'm sorry, could you repeat what you just said? A spa city? What is that?
> A: Let me explain. In 1998, archaeologists discovered the ancient spa city of Allianoi.
> B: What do you mean? Why did you call it a spa city?
> A: Because the city was famous for its bathhouses. Important Romans would visit the city to go to the bathhouses. That is why it is called The Spa City.
> B: Wow! Are the bathhouses still there?
> A: Yes and no.
> B: What do you mean by yes and no?
> A: Well, they are building a dam near Allianoi. So, to save the bathhouses, Turkish officials decided to rebury the site with sand! They want to save the bathhouses by keeping them buried under sand.

Exercise E. | Role-Playing

You may want to play the audio again and point out any special points relating to intonation or stress.

Exercise F. | Note-Taking

track 2-47

- Remind students that note-taking involves writing key words and phrases of the main ideas. They should not try to write complete sentences.
- Play the audio again.

Exercise G. | Discussion

- As an extra challenge, you can ask students to write as much of the conversation as they can without looking at the book. They can do this as a group, with one person taking the role of secretary.
- Then they can open their books to check their work.

Engage: Role-Playing

45 mins

(page 140)

WARM-UP

- **To introduce the idea of role-playing, you may want to use this activity.**
- **Prepare two role cards.**

Role card 1: You are a waiter in a restaurant. A customer is complaining to you about the food.

Role card 2: You are a customer in a restaurant. You are not happy with the food. Complain to the waiter.

- Choose two volunteers to come to the front of the class. Give one role card to each student.
- Then tell them to mime the conversation (using body language but no words). The rest of the class will try to guess the situation.
- When they have finished, you may ask them to try role-playing again, this time *with* words.
- Now brainstorm with the class what skills can be learned from role-playing. Your list may include the following:

  –How to react in different situations

  –Practice words and phrases appropriate to different situations

  –How to interact

  –How to ask for clarification

  –How to use appropriate body language

- Read the information in the box and compare their answers with the information contained there.

Exercise A.

- Pair students to read the conversation.
- Give tips on appropriate stress and intonation.
- Ask students to switch roles and read the conversation again (see TIP below).

TIP Demonstrate the "look up and speak" technique for reading dialogs. First, look down and read one sentence silently. Then look up and say the sentence while looking at your partner. Have students switch roles and read the dialog again using this technique.

Presentation Skills: Using Body Language

- Present the information in the box.
- Tell students to demonstrate each aspect of body language:

  Eye contact: look at your partner's eyes, but don't stare.

  Facial expression: smiling, frowning, looking puzzled, looking interested

  Posture: sitting straight, leaning over your book, looking downwards

  Movements: nodding, shaking your head, moving your hands or arms or shoulders

- Ask students to demonstrate how they would show interest in their partner's opinions through body language.
- Ask students to work in pairs. Student A reads one half of the dialog. Student B student responds using only body language.

Exercise B. | Creating a Dialog

Have students work in pairs to create their own dialogs.

Exercise C. | Role-Playing

Pairs of students can role-play their dialog for another pair of students or for the whole class.

> **IDEAS FOR . . . Expansion**
>
> Ask students to do some research about cultural differences in body language. How do people in different cultures use body language in conversations? Students may want to speak about their own cultures or a culture they know well.

A New View

Unit Theme

Unit 8 explores the topic of new developments in technology that are changing our views on medicine and architecture, as well as changing the way we live.

Think and Discuss *(page 141)*

5 mins

- Point out the unit title and the academic pathways.

- Ask students how the title might relate to the photo.

- Discuss question 1. Useful vocabulary: *muscles, bones, joints, skull, brain, nerves, skeleton, electric wires, send, receive, signals.*

- Discuss question 2. Write general topics on the board, for example: *medicine, communication, work, transport, education.* Then ask students for a specific example in each area.

- Discuss question 3. Possible topics could include: robots, artificial intelligence, artificial limbs.

Vocabulary Note

bionic (= a body, or part of a body, that is replaced by mechanical or electronic parts)

Exploring the Theme

15 mins

(pages 142–143)

The opening spread features a photo of a bionic arm and photos of possible future technological developments.

- Discuss the bionic arm. Ask: *What does cutting-edge mean?* (latest or most recent, very modern) *What can a bionic arm do? In what ways could a bionic arm be better than a human arm?*

- Ask students to describe each of the three photos on page 143 and read the information.

- Discuss questions 1–3. Ask: *What are the advantages of each development?*

IDEAS FOR . . . **Expansion**

Divide the class into four groups. Assign one technological development from this page to each group. In groups, students should brainstorm all the benefits of their innovation. Then each group will role-play a panel of experts or scientists who have developed this idea and present their innovation to the rest of the class. The other students will role-play journalists, doctors, and members of the public who have doubts about the new technology and will ask questions to try to find out the possible disadvantages.

Building Vocabulary

(page 144)

WARM-UP

The Lesson A target vocabulary is presented in the context of recent innovations in medical technology that can enhance physical abilities.

Ask students for some examples of how technology is used in medicine. For example, X-rays, MRI scans, keyhole surgery using scopes and cameras.

Exercise A. | Meaning from Context

track 2-48

- Have students describe each picture and say what these people are doing and how technology is helping them.
- Call on individuals to read each of the sentences. Then ask students to paraphrase each sentence in their own words or give examples that illustrate its meaning.

Vocabulary Note

cochlear (= relating to the inner cavity of the ear where the important nerve endings are found that enable us to hear)

Exercise B.

After checking the answers, ask students to work in pairs to quiz each other on the meaning of each word. Student A reads the definition and student B answers with the correct words. Then they switch roles.

Answer Key

1. command 2. device 3. signal 4. bionic 5. limb
6. artificial 7. control 8. communicate

Using Vocabulary

(page 145)

Exercise A.

- Ask students to describe the photo. What is the person in this photo trying to do?
- Tell students to work individually.

- Answer any question about extra vocabulary.
- As an extra challenge, tell students to complete the text without looking back at the previous page.

Vocabulary Note

volunteer (= offer to do something), nervous system (= system of nerves in the body), implant (= insert)

Answer Key

1. artificial 2. device 3. commands 4. controls 5. limb
6. bionic 7. communicates 8. signals

IDEAS FOR . . .   Checking Comprehension

Ask these additional questions about the passage or write them on the board.

1. What do these three devices have in common? (They are all examples of ways that technology is helping people with disabilities.)
2. How is the bionic arm different from the camera and the microphone? (The brain sends messages to the arm, but the camera and microphone send messages to the brain.)

Exercise B.

- Allow time for students to work individually to complete the sentences.
- Pair students to compare ideas.
- Discuss the ideas of student pairs as a class.

Answer Key

1. artificial/bionic 2. limbs 3. device 4. signals

Exercise C. | Self-Reflection

To help them answer this question, students may want to list the types of everyday tasks that someone would use a bionic arm or leg to accomplish.

Developing Listening Skills

(pages 146–147)

Pronunciation: Contractions with *Will*

- Introduce the information in the box.
- Explain that *will* is just one way of talking about the future in English. (Other ways are: *going to* + verb, simple present, and present continuous.)
- Demonstrate the difference between the full form and the contraction of *will* following a pronoun. For example: *I will* → *I'll*
- Play the audio and pause so that students can repeat.
- You may want to mention that contractions are also sometimes used with names and other nouns. For example: *The bus'll be faster than the train.* Contractions are not used with short answers. For example: *Will you take the bus tomorrow? Yes, I will.* (not: *Yes, I'll.*)

Exercise A.

- Have students practice in pairs. Then call on individuals to say each pair of sentences.
- For item 4, you may want to demonstrate the difference in pronunciation between *You like the book* and *You'll like the book.*
- Give a quick quiz to see if students can hear the difference between these pairs of sentences.

  I listen to the CD. / I'll listen to the CD.

  They look at the car. / They'll look at the car.

  You laugh at this photo. / You'll laugh at this photo.

Vocabulary Note

cloning (= creating an identical copy of an organism from a clone cell)

Exercise B.

Choose volunteers to read out their sentences.

Answer Key

1. They'll watch a movie about robots.
2. He'll get a bionic arm.
3. She'll clone her pet when it dies.

Before Listening

Prior Knowledge

Form groups and tell students to come up with as much information as they can about dinosaurs.

> **TIP** You may want to draw a chart on the board with three columns. The first column is for things we know about dinosaurs. The second column is for things we are not sure about. The third column is for things we want to know.

Listening: A Scientific Talk

Exercise A. | Listening for the Main Idea

- Allow time for students to read the statements.
- Play the audio while students choose their answers.
- Compare answers as a class.

Answer Key

b. The professor is giving a talk on cloning.

Exercise B. | Listening for Details

- Have students read the statements.
- Play the audio again. Then pair students to compare their answers.
- Play difficult sections of the audio again, if necessary, to clarify any answers.

Answer Key

1. c 2. b 3. a

IDEAS FOR . . . Checking Comprehension

Ask students these additional questions or write them on the board.

1. Why does the professor mention the film *Jurassic Park*? (Because it is about a scientist who clones dinosaurs.)
2. Why does the professor mention a photocopying machine? (To give an example of something that makes copies.)
3. Why is the student worried about cloning dinosaurs? (Because they might invade our cities and attack us or eat us.)
4. What problem with cloning technology does the professor mention? (It is very expensive.)

After Listening

Exercise A. | Self-Reflection

Form groups of students to discuss the questions.

> **TIP** Before discussing the self-reflection questions in exercise A, you may want to ask students to first write down one or two ideas individually. This will help them start their discussion more easily.

Exercise B. | Critical Thinking

Encourage students to think of as many possible answers as they can. Discuss the ideas as a class. Try to reach a consensus on what kinds of limits should be put on scientists.

45 mins

Exploring Spoken English
(pages 148–149)

Language Function: Describing Objects Using Adjectives

- Explain that adjectives are words used to describe things. They can come after the verb *be* (and some other verbs, such as *appear, seem, look, become*) or before the noun.

- Ask for some examples of adjectives. You may want to look back at one of the earlier readings in this unit and ask students to pick out all the adjectives.

- Make sure students understand that the word *object* in the heading refers to *things*, <u>not</u> the object of a sentence.

- Go over the information in the box.

track 2-51

Exercise A.

- Play the audio while students underline their answers.

- As extra practice, ask students to also identify the noun and the verbs.

- Check the answers before going on to exercise **B**. Note that item 3 has two adjectives.

- You may want to play the audio and pause for students to repeat.

Answer Key

1. The microphone is <u>small</u>.
2. Robots are <u>helpful</u>.
3. <u>Artificial</u> limbs are <u>difficult</u> to use.
4. The scientist is <u>excited</u>.
5. Dinosaurs are <u>extinct</u>.

Exercise B.

- Walk around the class while students practice to help with any pronunciation difficulties.

- As extra practice, ask students to replace the adjectives in these sentences with other adjectives that still make sense.

Exercise C.

- Allow time for students to work in pairs to complete the sentences.

- Check the answers before they practice. Note that some blanks may have more than one possible answer.

Answer Key

1. interesting; bionic 2. tiny; artificial

Grammar: The Future with *Will*

- Go over the information in the box.

- Emphasize the two different uses of *will*. Give some additional examples of each use.

- Point out that when we use *will*, the main verb does not change.

- Remind students of the contracted forms of *will* that they studied on page 146.

- You may want to teach question forms with *will* (*yes/no* and *wh-* questions) as these will come up in exercises **C** and **D**.

> **IDEAS FOR ... Extension**
>
> Brainstorm ideas for possible technological developments in the future. Write them on the board in the form of a spider diagram. You may want to assign one topic to each group. For example, transportation, communication, food, clothing, medicine, education, home. As a class, discuss which one is the most likely development in each category.

Exercise A.

- Check the answers by asking individuals to read out their sentences.

- As additional practice, ask students to identify the adjectives.

Answer Key

1. will grow 2. will help 3. will operate 4. will travel

Exercise B.

- Ask students to describe the picture.

- Allow time for students to choose their answers individually.

- Check the answers before they practice in pairs.

- Find out students' opinions about flying cars and robots.

- As an extra challenge, ask students to make up their own conversations about possible future technological developments.

Answer Key

1. will life be 2. will fly 3. will do 4. will clean 5. will be 6. will never 7. will be

Exploring Spoken English
(page 150)

track 2-52

Exercise C.

- Ask students to look at the photo and describe what is happening. What is the robot wearing? Why?
- Ask students to read the title and try to predict what the article will be about.
- Ask what students know about robots. Where are they used now? How do they help humans?
- Play the audio while students read the article.
- Allow students time to read silently and underline verbs with *will*.
- Check the answers as a class.
- Find out what information students found most surprising and why.

Answer Key

Robots <u>will</u> think, act, and communicate like humans. Are we ready?

A new group of robots <u>will</u> soon help us in our homes, schools, and offices. According to some robotics professors, in five or 10 years, robots <u>will</u> work in human environments. We <u>will</u> watch and communicate with our robots from our computers at work. Some robots may cook for us, fold the clothes, and babysit our children. They <u>will</u> also take care of our elderly parents.

Here are some good questions many people ask. What <u>will</u> these future robots look like? <u>Will</u> they change the way we communicate with each other? Are we ready for them?

Studies show that people want robots to act like humans. But we don't want them to look like humans! And, we don't want them to make mistakes. Engineers and scientists want to make robots that make us happy. They want to make sure they <u>will</u> help us and make us comfortable. In the future, we don't know if everyone <u>will</u> have a robot at home. But we do know that robots <u>will</u> be a part of our future.

Exercise D.

- Pair students to discuss the questions. Walk around as they practice and identify any problems with using *will*.
- Ask students for their answers and provide feedback on the use of *will*.
- Explain that the answers to these questions are all in the article.
- Ask a student to ask you the first question so that you can model the answer.
- Students who want an extra challenge can cover the article and try to answer from memory.

- Ask students to make additional questions about the article.

Answer Key

1. We will see robots in our homes, schools, and offices.
2. We will communicate with the robots from our computers.
3. Robots will cook, fold clothes, babysit our children, and take care of elderly parents.
4. Robots will work with us soon—in five to 10 years.
5. No, we don't want robots to look like humans.
6. Yes, we do want robots to act like humans.

Exercise E. | Self-Reflection

Encourage students to come up with as many possible answers as they can. Take a class vote on who would like a robot and who wouldn't. As an extension, conduct a class discussion on whether robots should be allowed in people's homes.

30–45 mins

Speaking *(page 151)*

Conducting a Survey

Exercise A.

- Read the information in the box. Ask if any students have ever conducted or been involved in a survey. Discuss how surveys are used in academic research.
- Ask students to read the questions and tell you what the survey is about (attitudes toward technology).
- Allow time for students to interview and be interviewed by three other students.

> **TIP** For exercise A, it may be helpful to ask students to stand up and walk around. When you clap your hands or make some other signal, they should stop and interview the person nearest to them.

Answer Key

Answers will vary.

Exercise B. | Critical Thinking

Encourage students to try to find patterns in the data they have collected. Which aspects of technology does everyone like or dislike, for example?

Exercise C. | Presentation

Tell students to form groups with students they have not worked with before. It may be necessary for you to form the groups in order to achieve this.

Viewing: Augmented Reality
(pages 152–153)

30 mins

Overview of the Video

The video is about how scientists are trying to combine virtual and real physical reality.

WARM-UP

Ask students to describe the photo. What are they doing? What is interesting or unusual about this phenomenon? Ask if any students have a cell phone and what they use it for. Ask if anyone has a smart phone or can explain what a smart phone is.

Before Viewing

Exercise A. | Discussion

- Allow time for students to discuss the questions in pairs.
- Discuss the answers as a class. Discuss what smart phones can do now and what they may be able to do in the future.

Exercise B. | Using a Dictionary

- Ask students to make example sentences for each of these words.
- Have students read their sentences to the class and see if the rest of the class agrees on the use of the word.

Exercise C.

track 2-53

- Allow time for students to complete their answers.
- Answer questions about any new vocabulary. For example: *bubbles, floating, GPS, compass, points of interest, powerful.*
- Ask students to say what aspects of smart phones they would use most often in their daily lives.

Answer Key

1. glasses 2. information 3. camera 4. screen 5. tool

Exercise D. | Predicting Content

Ask students to describe the photo. Draw attention to the information on the left which depicts what the woman is able to see with her glasses.

While Viewing

Exercise A.

- Play the video while students watch and take notes.
- Pair students to summarize the main ideas.

Exercise B.

- Give students time to read all the sentences before watching.
- Play the video again while students write their answers.
- Compare answers as a class and write them on the board.

Answer Key

1. future 2. information 3. environment 4. lost

Exercise C.

- Give students time to select their answers.
- Play the video or selected parts of the video again if necessary.

Answer Key

1. T 2. T 3. F 4. T

IDEAS FOR . . . Checking Comprehension

Ask students these additional questions, or write them on the board, and play the video again.

1. What can you see by using this new technology? (text, graphics, 3D images)
2. What kind of information can it give us? (maps, locations, facts)
3. What three types of people could benefit from this technology? (firefighters, pilots, and tourists)

After Viewing

Exercise A. | Collaboration

- Ask students to discuss their questions in groups.
- You may want to assign some of these questions for homework.

Exercise B. | Discussion

Advise each group to appoint one person as secretary to take notes on their ideas.

Building Vocabulary

(page 154)

30 mins

track 2-54

Meaning from Context

- Ask students to describe the photo. What do they think are the benefits of these vertical gardens?
- Play the audio while students read the article.
- Answer questions about any additional vocabulary. For example: *balcony, freshwater, pyramid.*

> **IDEAS FOR ... Checking Comprehension**
>
> Ask some general questions about the article.
>
> 1. What is similar about these three designs?
> 2. How are they different from modern skyscrapers?
> 3. What are the advantages of living in one of these structures?
> 4. What are the disadvantages?

Using Vocabulary

(page 155)

Exercise A.

- Allow time for students to complete their answers individually.
- As an extra challenge, ask students to complete the answers without looking back at the passage.
- Check the answers as a class.
- Write the answers on the board.

Answer Key

1. architect 2. Residents 3. vertical 4. farm 5. design 6. market 7. provide 8. create

Exercise B. | Collaboration

- Make sure every pair of students has a dictionary.
- Complete the first row of the chart as a class as an example.

- Allow time for students to work in pairs.
- Draw a chart on the board and choose volunteers to come to the board and write their answers.
- Note that *design, farm,* and *market* can be nouns or verbs.

Answer Key

Answers will vary.

Exercise C.

- Allow time for students to work in pairs.
- Remind students to use the target vocabulary as much as possible.
- Discuss the answers as a class.

Exercise D.

- Allow time for students to complete their answers individually.
- Ask volunteers to read out their sentences to the class to check their answers.
- As a follow-up, ask students to summarize the information in the passage using all of the new words.

Answer Key

1. architect 2. Farms 3. created 4. Residents 5. markets 6. design 7. provide 8. Vertical

> **IDEAS FOR ... Expansion**
>
> 1. Ask students to work in groups to design their own home of the future. They can draw a large diagram on a poster and label it using as many of the words studied in this unit as possible. The posters can be displayed on the walls of the classroom.
> 2. Ask students to find out more information about the vertical gardens in Singapore or one of the other designs mentioned in the passage. They can tell the class what they found out in the next lesson.

Developing Listening Skills
(pages 156–157)

45 mins

 Check the answers as a class. Ask students to explain why the false sentences are false.

Listening for Statements of Opinion
track 2-55

■ Introduce the information in the box and play the audio.

■ Ask students to repeat the examples.

■ Ask if students know of any other expressions for expressing opinions. For example: *From my point of view . . . I feel that . . . In my view. . .*

■ Ask students to match the sentence parts.

■ As a follow-up, ask students to complete the sentence stems with their own ideas on the theme of homes of the future.

Answer Key

Answers will vary.

Before Listening

 Predicting Content

Remind students of the importance of predicting content before listening.

Answer Key

The following topic should be checked: Transportation of the future will be different.

Listening: A Debate between Friends

 Exercise A. | Listening for Main Ideas
track 2-56

■ Discuss the differences between a formal debate and a debate between friends.

■ Ask students to describe the photo.

■ Allow time for students to read all the sentences.

■ Play the audio.

■ Compare answers as a class.

Answer Key

1. c 2. c

 Exercise B. | Listening for Details
track 2-56

■ Allow time for students to read the sentences.

■ Play the audio again.

Answer Key

1. T 2. T 3. F 4. T 5. F

Exercise C. | Checking Predictions
track 2-56

■ Refer students back to their answers on the previous page.

■ Play the audio again, if necessary.

After Listening

Exercise A. | Self-Reflection

■ Discuss what kind of criteria could be used to rank these items. What could make one of these more important than the others? For example: better for the environment, prevents pollution, makes life easier or cheaper, makes people healthier or happier.

■ You may want to assign one of these values to each group and then compare how the ranking differs between each group.

■ Remind students to use expressions for statements of opinion.

Answer Key

Answers will vary.

Student to Student: Showing Agreement and Disagreement

■ Present the information in the box.

■ Practice saying these expressions using appropriate intonation.

■ Add any further expressions that students know.

Exercise B. | Critical Thinking

■ Allow time for students to work in groups to discuss their opinions.

■ To promote more active disagreement, suggest that students take opposing views on each topic, even if they aren't expressing their true opinion.

■ For question 1, you may want to discuss and compare different ways to get information, such as the Internet, TV, and newspapers. Which are the most reliable, and why?

30 mins

Exploring Spoken English
(pages 158–159)

Grammar: The Future with *Be Going To*

- Go over the information in the box and practice the examples.

- Point out that *going to* doesn't change, but the verb *be* changes. Ask: *How many forms of the verb* be *are there? When do we use each form?*

- You may want to contrast *going to* with the information about *will* on page 149.

- Point out that in spoken English, *going to* is often pronounced as *gonna*.

> **IDEAS FOR . . . Practicing Grammar**
>
> Ask each student to write down one thing they are going to do next weekend on a slip of paper. Collect the slips and mix them up. Redistribute them so that every student has a different sentence. Then ask students to walk around the class and find the student who wrote their sentence. They should ask them for more details about their plans.

track 2-57

Exercise A.

- Ask students to describe the photo. What could this ear be used for?

- Play the audio while students read.

- Discuss the meanings of new words, such as *lab, heart, liver, surgeon.*

- Call on individual students to read aloud the verbs with *going to*. Ask them to identify the subject of each verb.

A: Did you watch TV last night? In the future, people who need a body part <u>are going to get</u> one from labs. Scientists <u>are going to grow</u> body parts from people's cells.

B: What was that again?

A: I said, in the future, scientists <u>are going to grow</u> body parts in the lab!

B: Wow! Really? They <u>are going to grow</u> body parts like ears and eyes in the lab?

A: Yes! Scientists <u>are going to grow</u> body parts that are called bioartificial organs.

B: I guess that will help people who are sick. In the future, if a person needs a heart, liver, or other organ, surgeons will order a bioartificial organ for them!

A: Isn't that amazing? In the future, do you think we <u>are going to live</u> a lot longer than we do today?

B: I don't know. But, I think life <u>is going to be</u> more interesting than it is today!

Exercise B.

If appropriate, play the audio again so that students can repeat each line paying attention to pronunciation, wordlinking, and intonation.

Exercise C.

- Allow time for students to write their answers.

- Check the answers by asking individuals to come and write their answers on the board.

- Have students read the sentences to each other in pairs.

- As an extension, ask students to make questions about each sentence. For example: *What are architects going to do?*

1. Architects are going to design vertical farms.
2. The scientist is going to grow body parts.
3. Robots are going to help us at home.
4. Scientists are going to clone extinct animals.
5. Vertical farms are going to provide vegetables in dry areas.

Exercise D.

- Discuss the illustrations with the class. What does each face represent? (A stage in the development of technology: smart phone, smart eyewear, smart contact lenses.)

- Ask students to read the conversation and choose their answers before practicing in pairs.

TIP Higher-level students can make up their own conversation on a similar theme. Remind them to use language for expressing opinions, and agreeing or disagreeing.

Answer Key

Answers will vary.

Critical Thinking Focus: Discussing Pros and Cons

Read the information in the box. What are the three steps that are described there? (1. Reflect on what we know; 2. Analyze the new information; 3. Make connections with what we know.)

Exercise E. | Critical Thinking

- Explain that pros are advantages and cons are disadvantages.
- Encourage students to add as many of their own ideas as they can.
- Draw the chart on the board and gather ideas from the whole class as you write.

Answer Key

Answers will vary.

Engage: Participating in a Debate *(page 160)*

45 mins

WARM-UP

- To introduce the idea of a debate, you may want to start with an easy topic, such as the pros and cons of eating meat, or of having a cell phone.
- Brainstorm arguments for and against your chosen topic and write them on the board.
- Discuss how you would go about finding further information and statistics to support each side of the issue.
- Model giving one side of the argument, using expressions for stating an opinion and listing your reasons with supporting facts and examples.
- Ask students what they noticed about your presentation.
- Ask students to practice in pairs using the information on the board. Each student will have just two minutes to present arguments for or against.

Presentation Skills: Debating

Read the information in the box about debating. Discuss each point with the class and ask why it is important.

Exercise A. | Planning a Debate

- Ask students to look at the photo and make sure they understand the concept of cloning. You may want to clarify whether they are going to discuss animal or human cloning, or both.
- Students can work in pairs or groups to complete the chart.

TIP It is a good idea for all students to complete both sides of the chart so that they have a better understanding of both sides of the issue.

Exercise B. | Preparing an Argument

- Students can work individually or in pairs to prepare their arguments.
- Make sure there are equal numbers of students in favor and against.
- Students may want to refer back to their notes from page 147 to get some ideas on cloning.

Exercise C. | Debate

- Have students form groups. Give each student in the group a number so that they know the order in which they will speak.
- Monitor students as they speak and check if they are using the expressions for giving an opinion.
- Follow up with a class discussion of the topic.
- Find out if any students changed their opinion after the debate. Ask them to explain why.

IDEAS FOR . . . Expansion

Ask students to do some research about cloning for homework. You may want to brainstorm questions that have come up during the debate. Write the questions on the board. Then assign a different question to each pair or group for homework.

CD 1

Unit 1: Same and Different
Lesson A
Building Vocabulary

Track 1-01   A.   Page 4

athlete
be a native of
carefree
foreign
home country
international
outgoing
traveler

Track 1-02   B. Meaning from Context   Page 4

Where are you from? For third culture kids, that is a hard question. Third culture kids don't live in their home country. They live in many countries. Third culture kids are the same as and different from other kids. Listen to their stories.

Hi, I am Marisa. I am a third culture kid. I am a native of the United States, but the United States is not my home country. My home countries are Singapore, the Philippines, and Korea. I am a world traveler and I speak many languages. I am the same as and different from other American kids. I like music and movies like other American kids. But I like international music and foreign movies instead of pop music and Hollywood movies.

Hello. I am Toshio. I am a third culture kid, too. I am a native of Japan, but Japan is not my home country. My home countries are South Africa and Zimbabwe. I am the same as and different from other Japanese kids. I like sports and I am an athlete like many Japanese boys my age. I play cricket but many Japanese boys play baseball. I am carefree and outgoing.

Developing Listening Skills

Track 1-03   Pronunciation: Word Stress   Page 6

Speakers stress certain words when they compare and contrast. The words *and, but,* and *both* are often stressed.

Example: *I have a twin sister. We are the same **and** we are different. We are **both** athletes. She likes to play tennis **but** I like to play soccer. We **both** like music. She likes pop music **but** I like rock music.*

Track 1-04   A.   Page 6

My twin brother and I are the same <u>and</u> we are different. We are from New Zealand. I live in my home country, <u>but</u> my twin lives in Ireland. We are <u>both</u> travelers. I like to visit places near my house, <u>but</u> my brother likes to travel to foreign countries. We are <u>both</u> big eaters. I like to eat meat, <u>but</u> he is a vegetarian. We <u>both</u> like to watch movies. I like to watch dramas, <u>but</u> he likes to watch action movies. We are <u>both</u> married. I have kids, <u>but</u> he doesn't have kids, yet. We are the same <u>and</u> we are different!

Listening: A Lecture

Track 1-05   A. Checking Predictions, B. Listening for the Main Idea, and C. Listening for Details   Page 7

Welcome back. Today, we continue with my lecture on identical twins. Please find a seat; we will begin shortly.

Identical twins. They are the same, *and* they are different. They come from the same egg that split into two. Why are they the same, and why are they different? Some researchers believe the similarities have to do with genetics. Others believe their parents teach them to be similar or different.

The story of the "Jim Twins" is an example of how twins can be so identical. In 1939, identical twin brothers were born. Two different families adopted the boys. Both families named the boys Jim. The two Jims met each other for the first time when they were 39 years old. They found that they are very similar. Both men are 6 feet tall and weigh 180 pounds. They both named their dogs Toy and they both took family vacations in St. Pete, Florida. They both had wives named Linda and then divorced. Their second wives were both named Betty. They both were fathers and named their sons James Alan. They both were police officers, liked to make things with wood, and they both got headaches. They grew up in different homes with different parents, but they are identical in many ways.

Not all identical twins are the same. Some twins are very different. For example, one twin is shy, but the other is outgoing. One twin is an athlete, but the other is an artist. One twin is a world traveler, but the other stays home. One twin is carefree, but the other is nervous.

So, twins can be the same in many ways and different in many ways. Are there any questions? If not, I'd like you to open your textbooks to page 146. Let's look at some more facts about twins.

Exploring Spoken English

Track 1-06   A.   Page 8

Conversation 1
A: Where are you from?
B: I'm from Brazil. Where are you from?
A: I'm from Japan. What do you do?
B: I am a student. What do you do?
A: I am a writer.
B: It's nice to meet you.
A: Nice to meet you, too.

Conversation 2
A: It's cold today, isn't it?
B: Yes! The weather is very different from yesterday.
A: Yes. Yesterday was so hot!
B: I know. And, today it is freezing. Very strange!
A: I agree.

Track 1-07   A.   Page 9

A: Hi, I am Tanya. What's your name?
B: My name is Anna. Where are you from?
A: I was born in Costa Rica, but I live in Russia. My mother is from Costa Rica, but my dad is from Russia. Where are you from?
B: We are from Canada. It is a nice place to live.
A: Were you born in Canada?
B: I was born in Canada, but my parents were born in Sweden.

Lesson B

Building Vocabulary

Track 1-08   A.   Page 14

alike
billion
Earth
female
male
one of a kind
special
typical

Track 1-09   B. Meaning from Context   Page 14

The world now has seven billion people. How are you and these seven billion others alike? Are you the same? Or are you one of a kind? Are you special? Within the seven billion people on Earth, who is the typical person? Listen to the facts about Earth's seven billion people.

A typical person . . .
makes less than $12,000 USD a year.
is a male.
has a cell phone.
is right-handed.
doesn't have a car.
does not have a bank account.
is 28 years old.

The typical person is a 28-year-old Han Chinese man. There are over 9,000,000 Han Chinese males in the world.

    Typical means different things in every country. A typical person in your home country is different from a typical person in another country. For example, a typical male in Holland is 5'11'', but a typical male in Peru is 5'4''. A typical Japanese female lives to be 86 years old, but a typical woman from Afghanistan lives to be 45 years old. A typical American uses 100 gallons of water a day at home, but a typical Ethiopian uses 2.5 gallons of water a day. Typical is different for each country.

Developing Listening Skills

Before Listening

Track 1-10   A. Using a Dictionary   Page 16

be in trouble
hang out with
impact
lazy
media
troublemaker

Listening: A Conversation

Track 1-11   A. Critical Thinking and B. Listening for Details   Page 17

A: Hi, Kathryn. Who was that woman?
B: Oh, hi, Mark. She is a doctor. I was talking to her about my twin sister, Carmen. Carmen is having a hard time at school. She is in trouble.
A: What's wrong with her? She is such a good student!

B: She *was* a good student. She was a hard worker, but lately she is lazy. She is not the same.
A: What do you mean?
B: Well, she is not a good listener now. She is a troublemaker. My parents are very angry.
A: What happened? She was such a good girl! Why is she so different now?
B: Well, the doctor said that many teenagers go through a change. She said that it is typical. For example, some kids were shy, but now as teens they are outgoing. Some kids were carefree, but now as teens they are nervous. Some kids were hard workers, but now as teens they are lazy.
A: Why is Carmen different now?
B: The doctor said we are who we are because of family, friends, media, and experiences in our lives. These things impact our lives.
A: What do you mean?
B: I mean, other people change us. We are our friends, family, and the people we hang out with. Carmen is friends with Brian, and Brian is not a good student. And now Carmen is a bad student. She is who she hangs out with. She is the same as Brian now.
A: I see. Hmm. What are you going to do?
B: I know she isn't happy. I am her sister. I'm going to talk with her about it. Tell her that she was a good student but now she isn't. Tell her that she was happy but now she isn't. She needs to find herself again.
A: You are a great sister.
B: She was a great sister, too. I want my sister back! Wish me luck!

Unit 2: Taking Risks
Lesson A

Building Vocabulary

Track 1-12   A.   Page 24

adventure
danger
exciting
extreme
popular
risky
seek
thrill

Track 1-13   B. Meaning from Context   Page 24

Adventure trips are very popular now. More and more people want to do something different and exciting on vacation. Some people seek danger, and some people get a thrill from adventure. These people often choose an extreme vacation. They parachute, cliff jump, and dive with sharks. Some people want a less risky adventure. They hike, raft, and cycle. There is an adventure for everyone, and they are all exciting! Listen to Jane talk about the kinds of adventure trips she goes on.

    I go on an adventure trip every year. I walk through the African Safari and I bike through the Grand Canyon. This is a photo from my favorite trip to Alaska. We take a small boat and get very close to the glaciers. They are beautiful.

Developing Listening Skills

Listening: A Radio Show

Track 1-14 A. Listening for Main Ideas and B. Listening for Details   Page 27

A: Welcome to Talk Radio 650 and today's episode of Taking Risks, where we talk about real life adventurers. We're your hosts, Jake Baker and Marie Smith, and in this show we will talk about the three finalists for *National Geographic*'s Adventurers of the Year contest.

B: Thanks, Jake, for that introduction. Now let's hear about these adventurers. The first one we'll talk about is climber Cory Richards. He is one of the first to climb Gasherbrum II in Pakistan, an 8,000 meter mountain, in the dead of winter!

A: That's right, Marie. As you can imagine, there are many risks to this climb even in perfect weather, but in the winter, there are many dangers like extreme temperatures and avalanches. Why does he take these risks?

B: Cory Richards says that he likes to climb in a simple way. He likes to feel that there is something bigger than him. He also says that climbers are always the mountain's guest.

A: Right. But, in this case the mountain was in a bad mood! While hiking up the mountain, Cory and his team were hit by an avalanche!

B: Amazing. And, believe it or not, he said he would go back again! He said that if you love something you don't just do it once.

A: Incredible! The next explorers we will talk about are two men from Nepal, Lakpa Tsheri Sherpa and Sano Babu Sunuwar, with a very different adventure.

B: Yes, they are the first ones to climb Mount Everest, then paraglide from the top of Mount Everest for as long as possible, bicycle to a river, kayak across the Indian/Nepali border, and finally paddle the Ganges River to the Indian Ocean.

A: Sano had never climbed before, so he felt that climbing Mount Everest was the hardest part. He said that it was really hard to breathe.

B: And for Lakpa, he didn't know how to swim. The kayaking part of the trip was very scary for him.

A: Incredible. Why did they do this adventure?

B: Believe it or not, they both said they did it for fun! They didn't do it to set a record or become famous. They just wanted adventure. They said that without adventure you don't feel real life.

A: So, these men all take the risks because they seek adventure. It's as simple as that.

B: Thank you for listening to our show today. And we want to thank Cory, Sano, and Lakpa for sharing their incredible stories with us.

Exploring Spoken English

Track 1-15   Pronunciation: The Third Person Singular   Page 30

The *s* at the end of a verb in the third person singular of the present tense has three different sounds: /s/, /z/, or /iz/. Here are the rules.

/s/ sound after these final sounds: /f/, /k/, /p/, /t/

Examples: He hikes. She paints. He surfs.

/z/ sound after vowels, and these final sounds: /l/, /m/, /n/, /r/, /th/, /v/, /d/

Examples: She plays. He goes. She swims. He paraglides. She skis. He snowboards.

/iz/ sound after these final sounds: /s/, /sh/, /ch/, /z/, /j/. The /iz/ sound is pronounced as a separate syllable.

Examples: He watches. She fixes. He washes. She fishes.

Track 1-16   A.   Page 30

climbs
kayaks
skis
snowboards
swims
hikes
surfs
watches
bikes
bungee jumps

Track 1-17   B.   Page 30

A: Hi, Sarah.

B: Hi, Mary. What are you doing this weekend?

A: I'm going to my friend Maria's house. She lives at the beach. I visit her every summer.

B: Fun. What do you do there?

A: Well, Maria likes extreme sports. I don't get a thrill from danger, so I just watch her take the risks!

B: Really? Cool! What does she do?

A: Well, she surfs, she cliff jumps, she kayaks, and she rock climbs.

B: Interesting! Does she do any winter sports?

A: Yes, in the winter she skis and snowboards.

B: She really likes danger!

A: Yes, she does. It is fun to watch her go!

Lesson B

Building Vocabulary

Track 1-18   A.   Page 34

act
discoveries
explore
explorer
information
make a fortune
needs
satisfy

Track 1-19   B. Meaning from Context   Page 34

Nalini Nadkami doesn't have a normal job. She is an explorer and her office is the rainforest. Her job can be risky. She hangs from ropes, hundreds of feet above the ground, in Costa Rica's Monteverde Cloud Forest. She learns about the plants at the top of the forest trees.

Eugenie Clark is another explorer. Her job can be risky, also. Some people call her the "Shark Lady." She learns about how sharks act and live. This information helps us know more about ocean animals.

There are many kinds of explorers. Some explore to satisfy our needs such as food and water. Some look for new information, or to make a fortune. Some search to set a record, find something new, and become famous for their discoveries. And, some explore to make the world a better place. These explorers risk their lives every day so that we can learn more about our planet.

Developing Listening Skills

Listening: A Conversation

Track 1-20   A. Listening for the Main Idea, B. Listening for Details, and C. Checking Predictions   Page 37

Marcus: Hi, Rebecca. What are you reading?

Rebecca: About this amazing woman, Emma Stokes. She's an explorer for *National Geographic*.

Marcus: What does she do?

Rebecca: She helps protect areas where animals that are in danger live.

Marcus: Interesting!

Rebecca: Yes, definitely interesting and adventurous, but really risky at times. She risks her life to do this job, but she loves it.

Marcus: What are some of the dangers?

Rebecca: Well, there was this time when her group had set up camp and then in the middle of the night, she woke up to screaming and big heavy footsteps.

Marcus: What was it?

Rebecca: Elephants! They didn't know they set up their camp in the middle of an elephant nest.

Marcus: Wow! Was she hurt?

Rebecca: No, luckily!

Marcus: What else does she do?

Rebecca: Well, she discovered 125,000 lowland gorillas in an unexplored region of Congo.

Marcus: That's a big discovery!

Rebecca: Yes, and it was very good news. Many people thought these gorillas were endangered.

Marcus: That's funny. It would be hard to miss 125,000 gorillas!

Rebecca: Well, that's the thing; the area was flooded, and therefore it was unexplored. So, Emma and her team fought their way through a thick forest. They had to cut tree limbs just wide enough to squeeze through.

Marcus: Rough trip! Where did they sleep?

Rebecca: Since the forest was so thick, they had to sleep in beds hung from trees.

Marcus: I guess it was worth it if they found 125,000 gorillas.

Rebecca: Yes, it does sound like a lot, but she says in the article that number can decrease very quickly. For example, if a company wants to cut the trees down or if the area gets hit by sickness, then the gorillas are in danger.

Marcus: Wow, that's terrible. I'd like to read the story. Where can I find it again?

Rebecca: It's on nationalgraphic.com. There are lots of great stories about other explorers on that site.

Unit 3: Enjoy the Ride!
Lesson A

Building Vocabulary

Track 1-21   A. Using a Dictionary   Page 44

commute
convenient
crowded
passenger
pedestrian
safe
share
vehicle

Track 1-22   B. Meaning from Context   Page 44

Narrator: How do you commute? There are many ways to travel. A bus, a car, and a train are usual ways to move from one place to another. There are many other vehicles, too. Read how these people get around in their countries.

Bora: I am Bora, and I am from Cambodia. In my village we make our own trains. We call them *norries*. A *norry* has a wooden frame, a bamboo floor, and a small engine. The *norry* goes on a train track. The passengers jump off when a real train comes!

Ana: I am Ana, and I am from Colombia. I commute by a cable car in the sky. My city has many hills. The cable car helps move the people throughout the city.

Ling: I am Ling, and I am from China. I bicycle to work. Cars, bikes, and pedestrians share the road. It is very crowded, but it is convenient and safe.

Developing Listening Skills

Track 1-23   Pronunciation: *There is* and *There are*
Page 46

When people speak English quickly, they don't always pronounce every word fully. In fast speech, the phrases *there is* and *there are* are often blended together.

There is becomes *There's* and is pronounced: [therez]

There are is pronounced: [therere]

Listen to the sentences. Pay attention to the blended sounds.

Careful Speech	Fast Speech
There's a car.	Thereza car.
There's an airplane.	Therezan airplane.
There are many vehicles.	Therere many vehicles.
There are many pedestrians.	Therere many pedestrians.

Before Listening

Track 1-24   Page 46

The mountain music festival is a lot of fun! There are so many interesting bands and people. The best way to get there is to go by car. But you can get to the music festival by other modes of transportation, too. First take the train to Moorestown. The train takes about three hours. Second, get on the #9 bus to Hill Ridge City. The bus takes about 45 minutes. Then, find a taxi to take you to the top of the mountain. The taxi ride is only about 20 minutes. Finally, walk a half a mile to the festival.

Listening: An Interview

Track 1-25   A. Listening for Main Ideas and B. Listening for Details   Page 47

A: Today, we are talking about interesting ways to travel. We have Maria McNeal with us. She is a journalist and writes a monthly article titled, "Trains and Tuk-Tuks." Maria travels to many interesting places by any means possible. Thanks for coming today, Maria.

B: Thanks for having me.

A: Maria, tell us about your article.

B: "Trains and Tuk-Tuks" is about getting from one place to another using any vehicle.

A: What are some interesting vehicles you use?

B: Well, I ride on all kinds, but one interesting one is a dogsled.

A: Really! Do people really use those?

B: Yes. People use them in cold places like northern Canada and Finland. They are a convenient way to travel in the snow.

A: And fun, too, I bet!

B: Yes, they are a lot of fun. Another vehicle is a *tuk-tuk.*

A: Ahh, yes. Your article has the word *tuk-tuk* in the title. What are *tuk-tuks,* and where do you use them?

B: *Tuk-tuks* are small vehicles. There are many kinds of *tuk-tuks.* Some have workers on foot that pull them, some have workers on bicycles that pull them, and some *tuk-tuks* have motors. Many people in Asia use them.

A: Are they safe?

B: Yes. I ride them all the time. I think they are safer than the bus.

A: The bus? I ride buses all the time, and I think they are very safe.

B: Well, that's if you ride *in* them. I ride on the top!

A: On top? Where do people ride on top of buses?

B: In many countries, but I often ride on top of the bus in Nepal.

A: Why?

B: Many buses are crowded with people, chickens, goats. I want fresh air, and so I ride on top.

A: Do other people ride there, too?

B: Oh, yes. It can be like a party up there sometimes!

A: Well, I will remember that the next time I am in Nepal! In fact, I'm going there next month. I really want to go to Annapurna. Any suggestions on how to get there?

B: Well, from Kathmandu, take a taxi to the bus station. Get on the bus marked for Pokhara. Again, I recommend the top of the bus!

A: Yes, I'll remember that!

B: Second, stay a night in Pokhara and get prepared for your trek. Buy water and supplies and rest up!

A: OK.

B: Finally, in the morning, take a *tuk-tuk* to the base of the mountain and start climbing!

A: Great. Thanks for the advice. And, thank you so much for joining us today. Best of luck on your next trip.

B: Thank you!

Lesson B

Building Vocabulary

Track 1-26   A. Using a Dictionary   Page 54

destination
get around
lie down
machine
miles/kilometers per hour
modern
old-fashioned
take it easy

Track 1-27   B. Meaning from Context   Page 54

A bus, a car, a train? How old-fashioned! We want something new! Read about some modern ways to get around town.

Personal Jet Pack: This machine takes you up above the vehicles below. You can fly! There are not many of these in the world, but maybe in the future we will all fly!

Self-Driving Car: Sleep, read, lie down while driving? You can in this self-driving car. A computer drives the car and you take it easy in the back seat.

Maglev Train: This is a train that doesn't touch the tracks. It gets you to your destination in record time. There is a Maglev Train in Shanghai, China. It takes passengers from Shanghai airport to downtown. It travels at 431 kilometers per hour.

Listening: A Conversation

Track 1-28   A. Listening for the Main Idea and B. Listening for Details   Pages 56–57

Tom: Oh, hi, Jen! Welcome back! How was your trip?

Jen: Wonderful! I had a great time.

Tom: Tell me about it. Where did you go? What did you do?

Jen: Well, I traveled all around the world and saw the most amazing things.

Tom: Tell me about a few.

Jen: Well, the zorbs and the zip lines were my favorites.

Tom: Wait a minute, now I really need to hear more. First, what is a zorb?

Jen: It's a large ball. You get inside the zorb, and you roll anywhere you want! In New Zealand, people ride in Zorbs for fun.

Tom: Wow, what a way to get around!

Jen: Yes, it's really fun. It goes on land or water. It is an amazing feeling!

Tom: I want to try that. How about the zip line? What is it, and where did you do it?

Jen: I did it in Costa Rica. You need to climb up to the top of the trees and then get into a safety belt that is connected to a cable. Then, you jump off and glide along the cable.

Tom: I bet that is a great view!

Jen: Yes, it's beautiful. You see everything from up there.

Tom: Do you feel safe?

Jen: Yes, for both the Zorb and the zip line you need to wear a helmet, so it is very safe.

Tom: Well, I know what I want to do on my next trip!

Unit 4: Unusual Destinations
Lesson A

Building Vocabulary

Track 1-29   A. Using a Dictionary   Page 64

breathtaking
get away
relax
secluded
spot
unknown
unusual
vacation

Track 1-30   B. Meaning from Context   Page 64

A: Where do you like to go on vacation? Do you like to go to a popular place or an unusual spot? Listen to these two people talk about their favorite destinations.

B: My favorite spot is Ochheuteal Beach, Cambodia. Not many people know about this beach. It is quiet and I can relax there.

There are parts of the beach that are completely secluded. I don't like to go to tourist destinations, so this beach is perfect for me.

C: I like to travel to unknown places. My favorite place to get away is Spencer Glacier in Alaska. In this photo, we are very close to the glaciers. They are breathtaking!

Listening: A Presentation

Track 1-31 A. Listening for Main Ideas and B. Listening for Details   Page 67

A: We are about to begin. Please sit down. Welcome to the 2013 Travel Convention: Unusual Destinations. Our first speaker is Tom Jenkins. He travels around the world and writes blogs and books about his adventures. His new book, *The Real Countryside,* is in bookstores now. Please help me welcome Tom Jenkins.

B: Thank you. Thank you, it's nice to be here today. Since this convention is about unusual destinations, I thought I would tell you about my recent vacation to Southeast Asia. I like to travel to unusual places. The unknown spots can be the most breathtaking. In Southeast Asia, Hong Kong, Bangkok, and Singapore are popular spots, but I like to go to the unknown destinations within a country—the secluded spots.

I have some pictures to show you so that you can see some of the views. I started my trip in Sumatra, Indonesia. Here I am walking through a rice field. The view is spectacular. There are many rice paddies like this one in Southeast Asia, but most travelers don't leave the cities to see the countryside.

After Indonesia, I went to Thailand. There are many travelers on Thailand's beaches, but I like to go to the secluded beaches. These beaches are peaceful and relaxing. Here I am relaxing on Koh Lipe. I am eating dinner with my friends.

Nepal was my last destination. I like to hike the Himalayan Mountains. The mountains are serene. Here I am hiking up the Langtang trail. Isn't the view spectacular?

I hope these pictures inspire you to walk the road less traveled and to see the real countryside. It is worth the trip!

Exploring Spoken English

Track 1-32 A.   Page 70

Conversation 1
A: What are you doing?
B: I'm reading a book on South Africa.
A: What did you say?
B: I'm reading a book on South Africa. I'm going to Cape Town next month.

Conversation 2
A: Do you want to have dinner now?
B: No, I'm planning my vacation.
A: Did you say you're planning your vacation?
B: Yes, I leave next week!

Lesson B

Building Vocabulary

Track 1-33 A. Meaning from Context   Page 74

There are many breathtaking places on Earth. Some of them are natural places and others are manmade attractions. From very old to very modern, we recommend the following spectacular manmade destinations.

Manmade islands of Dubai

These are manmade islands off the coast of Dubai. They are several miles wide. One group of islands is in the shape of palm trees, and another group is in the shape of a world map. They are resort islands. Many people visit them each year.

Petra, Jordan

This city is 2,500 years old and is on many travelers' lists for unusual destinations. It is in the middle of the Jordanian desert. There are many beautiful temples and monuments. It is recommended for travelers seeking an unknown vacation spot.

Wat Rong Khun, Thailand

There are many temples in Thailand, but the Rong Khun, named The White Temple, is spectacular. It is just outside Chang Rai in northern Thailand. This unusual temple is all white. It has a mix of modern and old styles together.

SkyPark, Singapore

SkyPark is located on top of three tall buildings. It overlooks the beautiful city of Singapore. With restaurants, a large swimming pool, and a museum of modern art, there is something for everyone. The view is breathtaking!

Developing Listening Skills

Listening: A Group Conversation

Track 1-34 A. Checking Predictions, B. Listening for Main Idea, C. Listening for Details, and D. Making Inferences   Pages 76–77

A: Hey, sorry I'm late. What's going on? What's everyone looking at?
B: Oh, Maria has her pictures from her vacation. She's telling us about her trip.
A: Where did she go?
B: She went to an ice hotel in Swedish Lapland.
A: Did you say ice hotel?
B: Yes, let's listen.
Maria: . . . . You know me, I'm always seeking unusual destinations. This year it was definitely unusual! The ICEHOTEL is a hotel made from ice and snow. It's in Lapland, about 200 kilometers north of the Arctic Circle. In November, when there is no sun, snow builders and artists from around the world come together to make the hotel. They spray snow onto steel walls and after they freeze, they take the walls away and the snow walls stay up. Each year, the design is different. Can you believe they design a new hotel each winter! This year was ICEHOTEL number 22, and there were 47 rooms. The hotel is open from December to April. In the spring, the sun comes out and the snow melts. Then they start to think about next year's hotel.
B: What's it like inside? What do you sleep on?
Maria: Well, it's very cold but comfortable. The temperature stays between -5 and -8 degrees Celsius. You dress in warm clothes and a hat and it's not that bad. At night, you sleep in a warm sleeping bag on a special bed of snow, ice, and reindeer skins. All the furniture is made of ice, and there is spectacular ice art all around the hotel. There is a warm part of the hotel. The bathrooms and showers are in that part. In the morning, they give you hot lingonberry juice in your bed, and then you go to the sauna before breakfast at the ICEHOTEL. I recommend that you only sleep one night in the ICEHOTEL. There is a warm hotel nearby.

A: Wow! What an adventure!

Maria: Yes, it was a spectacular natural and manmade attraction! It was a good mix!

B: Do you have pictures?

Maria: Oh, yes. In this picture, I am sitting at the table in the restaurant. In this picture, my sister is relaxing on the bed. In this picture, my sister is looking at the ice art.

A: Great pictures. Thanks for sharing!

After Listening

Track 1-35   Pronunciation: Reduction of *-ing*   Page 77

When people speak English quickly, they don't always pronounce every word fully. In fast speech, the *-ing* in the present continuous often gets reduced. Listen to the sentences. Pay attention to the reduction of the *-ing*.

Careful Speech	Fast Speech
I am looking at the view.	I'm lookin' at the view.
We are relaxing on the beach.	We're relaxin' on the beach.
They are eating breakfast.	They're eatin' breakfast.

Exploring Spoken English

Track 1-36   B.   Page 78

A: Hi, Keiko? It's Alex. Are you working now?

B: No, I'm taking my vacation this week.

A: Where are you?

B: I'm on Easter Island. I'm on a group tour with 15 other people.

A: Wow! Are you having a good time?

B: Yes, I'm learning a lot about the island, and I'm having a lot of fun.

A: What are you doing right now?

B: I'm hiking up a big mountain.

A: Are you seeing beautiful views?

B: Yes, I'm standing on a bridge that overlooks the island's famous statues. It's a spectacular view!

 CD 2

Unit 5: Our Changing World
Lesson A

Building Vocabulary

Track 2-01   A. Using a Dictionary   Page 84

become
competition
develop
entertainment
hope
practice
skill
young

Track 2-02   C. Meaning from Context   Page 84

Shaolin Kung Fu Master: Hu Zhengsheng

When Hu Zhengsheng was a young boy, he loved to watch kung fu films. He saw kung fu as a form of entertainment.

Hu went to Shaolin Temple when he was 11 years old. He became a servant to one of the teachers. He practiced martial arts for many years and learned the movements for self-defense and good health.

Hu started a small school. Today, his school has 200 students. He teaches the students traditional Shaolin kung fu. His students sleep in cold rooms. Every day they practice kung fu very early in the morning, even in very cold weather. It is hard, but Hu knows this will help his students develop the skills they need in life. It will also help them become good at Shaolin kung fu.

Using Vocabulary

Track 2-03   B.   Page 85

What is Shaolin kung fu? Where did it come from? There is an old story in China. It says that many years ago the monks at Shaolin Temple learned special exercises. These exercises were hard and took a lot of practice. Later, the monks named these exercises "kung fu." The monks used kung fu to defend themselves from people who wanted to fight them. Today, monks still practice kung fu, but they do not use it to fight. Many young boys and girls study kung fu near the Shaolin Temple. They are learning skills that will help them find good jobs. Some students hope to become movie stars. Some students want to win kickboxing competitions. In the past, kung fu was used for war, but today it is a form of entertainment.

Developing Listening Skills

Track 2-04   Pronunciation: Using Intonation to Ask for Something or Make a Request   Page 86

When we ask a question or make a request, our voice rises at the end of the request.

Examples:

Could you tell me where the kung fu class is, please?

Excuse me, can you teach me that skill again?

Would you mind helping me practice?

Will you drive me to the competition today?

Listening: A Lecture

Track 2-05   A. Listening for the Main Idea, B. Listening for Details, and C. Checking Predictions   Page 87

Good morning. Today I'd like to speak to you about how our world is changing. Often the changes are small. The changes take place over time, so we don't always notice them. The changes I am talking about usually happen within our traditions.

One example is the Native American pow-wow. A pow-wow is a special gathering of Native Americans. Every year, Native Americans get together at pow-wows to eat, sing, dance, renew old friendships, and make new friends. They wear traditional clothes, eat traditional food, and dance traditional dances. Most of the dances have been passed down from generation to generation. But some of the dances are newer and are changing. Dancing at pow-wows is very important. In the past, it was never done for money. However, in many pow-wows today, dancing is done for money or to win competitions.

Another change is in the music. Newer songs are being brought in, and older songs are being left out. Native American music used to be played on a large drum by a group of men who also sang traditional songs. However, at a pow-wow today you might see a woman in the group playing the drum with the men.

Another change in tradition is that some Native Americans stay in hotels instead of camping out at the pow-wows, or they eat in restaurants instead of cooking over an open fire at the pow-wow. Finally, modern pow-wows are no longer only for Native Americans. Today, both Native Americans and non-Native Americans participate in pow-wows. They all meet to dance, sing, socialize, and honor Native American culture. Regardless of these changes, a pow-wow is still a special time when families get together to honor the past and celebrate the future.

Exploring Spoken English

Track 2-06   Page 88

A: Why did you start your own pastry shop?
B: I wanted to continue the tradition of baking French pastry. I thought the younger generation was eating too much fast food. I wanted them to eat traditional dessert such as our French pastries.
A: Where did you learn to bake French pastries?
B: Oh! I helped my father when I was young. I worked in his pastry shop.
A: How long did you work in his pastry shop?
B: Well, let's see . . . I baked with my father for 10 years.
A: Wow! Why so long?
B: I liked working in the shop and talking to different people. I learned a lot while I was there.
A: Annie, what you have done is very important. People like you keep our traditions for the next generation.
B: Thanks! I hope so!

Track 2-07   B.   Page 89

The clothes people wear today are different from the clothes in the past. Many years ago, the clothes looked much different. For example, in the 1900s, women wore long dresses and hats. It is interesting to see how the clothes we wear change over time. Change is a part of our lives. It occurs in our traditions, clothes, work, and transportation. What we think is beautiful today, we might not think is beautiful tomorrow. What do you think clothes will look like in the future? Will the clothes of tomorrow look like the clothes of today?

Lessons A & B

Viewing

Track 2-08   B. Using a Dictionary   Page 93

This video shows a pow-wow in South Dakota. You see Native Americans dancing. You hear Native Americans singing to drums. You also listen to a Native American named Buck Spotted Tail from the Sioux reservation talk. He talks about how he learned to dance like his ancestors. He also tells how he gradually changed the way he dances to a more contemporary style. Buck Spotted Tail talks about why it is important for Native American families to get together at pow-wows. It is where they have fun and learn to sing and dance.

Native Americans also learn more about their traditions at pow-wows. Buck Spotted Tail says that a pow-wow is a way to bring people together in a big celebration.

Lesson B

Building Vocabulary

Track 2-09   A. Meaning from Context   Page 94

A Need for Lifestyle Change

With 165 million people in Pakistan, there is a shortage of electricity. During the day, the electricity often goes out. Sometimes the electricity goes out for 12 hours or more! The government is asking shops to close early to save energy. Shop owners are not happy. They say customers do not want to shop in the day when there is no electricity because it is too hot. The government also has new rules for weddings and banks. Pakistani wedding celebrations must finish earlier instead of ending after midnight. Government offices and banks now have a two-day weekend, instead of a one-day weekend.

A Change in Lifestyle Means More Energy

Because of the new rules, people are slowly changing their habits. They are adapting to a new lifestyle. For example, now they shop before 8:00 P.M. Celebrations end earlier and people are more careful of how they use electricity. This change of lifestyle is very important and has helped the government save energy.

Developing Listening Skills

Track 2-10   Pronunciation: The Intonation of *Wh-*Questions   Page 96

When we ask a question with *what, when, where,* and *why,* the speaker's voice first rises and then falls at the end of the sentence.

What do customers want?

When do shop owners close their shops?

Where is the shortage of electricity?

Why don't customers like to shop in the day?

Track 2-11   A.   Page 96

A: What are you doing?
B: Oh, I'm just thinking.
A: Why do you look so serious?
B: I can't decide if I want to go to college or stay home and work with my family. What do you think?
A: Hmm, what do your parents say?
B: They want me to be happy, but I know they need me here, too.
A: That's a hard decision. When do you need to decide?
B: Well, the college applications are due in two weeks, so I need to decide soon.
A: Talk to your parents. They can help you decide.

Listening: A Short Documentary

Track 2-12 A. Listening for the Main Idea and B. Listening for Details   Page 97

Sami herders call their work *boazovázzi*, which means "reindeer walker." Many years ago, the herders followed the fast animals on foot or wooden skis. But times have changed. Today, the herders use special vehicles and snowmobiles to move the large herds. Nils Peder, a herder, says the Sami lifestyle is changing. Herding families now live in modern homes with Internet and television. Cell phones and texting is now a part of their life. Herders wonder if these outside cultural influences will change the young Samis. What path will young Samis choose? Will they choose a different lifestyle and decide to study and move to larger towns? Or will they stay in their community and become herders like their parents and grandparents? If reindeer herding disappears, Sami traditions may disappear too.

Exploring Spoken English

Track 2-13 A.   Page 98

Venice, Italy, is changing. For hundreds of years, Venice has been flooding. But the flooding is getting worse. When it floods, water is everywhere! As a result, Venetians have made many changes to their lifestyles. First of all, every Venetian has boots in his or her closet. Also, when it floods, people have learned to walk on the high footpaths that are set up in the city. Venetians use boat timetables instead of bus timetables. And, when they want to move from their apartments, they do not use trucks to move their furniture—instead they use boats. Unfortunately, many people are leaving Venice. They cannot adapt to the flooding and lifestyle changes.

Track 2-14 B.   Page 99

A: I was in San Francisco last week.
B: Why did you go there?
A: My family lives there, and I wanted to visit them.
B: Wow! You are so lucky! San Francisco is such an interesting city. I was there two years ago. I remember how beautiful the Golden Gate Bridge was.
A: I know! I love San Francisco! But things are different. The city has changed.
B: How has it changed?
A: Well, some of the older buildings are not there. People want to build newer and safer homes. They want homes that will not fall during an earthquake.
B: Did you see any other changes?
A: Yes. San Francisco is more international. There are more people from all over the world living in San Francisco now.
B: So, San Francisco really has changed in many ways.
A: Yes, it has. But there is one thing that is still the same—the Golden Gate Bridge! I hope it never changes.

Unit 6: Facing Challenges
Lesson A

Building Vocabulary

Track 2-15 A. Using a Dictionary   Page 104

accomplishment
afraid
ambition
challenge
climb
encourage
inspire
professional

Track 2-16 D. Meaning from Context   Page 104

Blind Ambition

Erik Weihenmayer lost his vision when he was 13 years old. He did not let being blind stop him from learning how to ski, mountain bike, and climb mountains. Erik became a professional athlete and continued his education. He became an elementary school teacher. He taught classes with up to 30 students in them. His other accomplishments include climbing the tallest mountains in all seven continents. He even climbed Mount Everest! He has inspired and guided blind Tibetan teenagers to 21,500 feet on Mount Everest. Erik has also led both blind and sighted students on hikes through the Andes. Erik must be well prepared and in good physical shape to achieve his ambitions. He is also a motivational speaker who encourages others and is successful because he is not afraid of any challenge.

Using Vocabulary

Track 2-17 A.   Page 105

A: Did you read the article on Erik Weihenmayer? Isn't he a fascinating person?
B: Yes, he really is! Imaging being blind and climbing a mountain!
A: Even for people who can see, climbing a mountain is very difficult.
B: You know, I was really surprised to learn that he is also a teacher and a professional athlete.
A: People like Erik really inspire people all around the world. Did you know that he is not the only person with a disability who has done amazing things?
B: Yes! I read about Helen Keller in school. She was blind, deaf, and could not speak. Helen Keller became famous because of all the accomplishments she had in her lifetime.
A: Right! But people who have disabilities are not the only people who face challenges. We all have difficulties in our lives. We face challenges at home, at work, at school, and in relationships.
B: I agree. Do you think challenges are good for us?
A: Yes, I do. I think if a person is not afraid and has ambition, then he or she can overcome most of life's challenges. I believe that challenges make us stronger.
B: You are so right! I think that people like Erik Weihenmayer and Helen Keller really encourage others to be brave and face life's challenges and never give up!

Developing Listening Skills

Listening: A Presentation

Track 2-18 A. Listening for Main Ideas, B. Listening for Details, and C. Checking Predictions for Details Page 106

Today's motivational presentation is about two people who are special, who inspire others. They are both very motivated mountain climbers. They like to climb very tall mountains.

They even like to climb in the snow and ice! But they are different from other climbers. They are different because they have disabilities. Erik Weihenmayer is blind, and Chad Jukes lost his right leg to an injury. Both Erik and Chad are very active. They go rock climbing, hiking, and ice climbing as much as they can. Chad also loves to ride his bike in the mountains. Erik and Chad do a lot of practicing before they climb difficult mountains and ice falls. For example, before Erik and Chad climbed Bridal Veil Falls, they got as much information as they could about it. This helped Erik to "see" where he would be climbing and what he would be doing in his mind. Chad prepared for the climb by practicing with a special prosthesis. It replaces his lost leg and was designed especially for use on the ice. Climbing ice is dangerous. Once, Erik was injured when he was hit in the shoulder with a big piece of ice. As Chad says, there is always the possibility that something bad will happen on a climb. But they do everything they can to stay as safe as possible. You may ask, "Why do they do what they do?" Well, Erik enjoys facing challenges and solving problems. Chad's message is to stay active and do everything you can to live a happy life. Though each one has a challenge, they both believe that they can do anything. They do not let their disabilities stop them. They want to show the world that they are able to overcome the many different challenges that life gives. Both Erik Weihenmayer and Chad Jukes are two very special people who inspire many people around the world.

After Listening

Track 2-19   Pronunciation: The Simple Past Tense -ed Endings   Page 107

Regular verbs in the simple past tense that end in -ed have three different pronunciations. In this section, we will learn about the /d/ sound.

-ed has a /d/ sound after these final sounds: /b/, /g/, /l/, /m/, /n/, /r/, /v/, /w/, /y/, or /z/

Examples: plan → plan**ed** → plan/**d**/, live → live**d** → live/**d**/

Track 2-20   Page 107

1. inspired
2. allowed
3. answered
4. climbed
5. challenged
6. cleaned
7. encouraged
8. enjoyed
9. listened

Exploring Spoken English

Track 2-21   D.   Page 110

World Famous Deaf Musician Inspires All Artists

Evelyn Glennie is a famous percussionist and composer. Like every musician, Evelyn has a challenging job. As a young musician, she spent hours and hours practicing and learning different musical instruments. And, because she wanted to be a composer as well, she spent even more hours learning music theory and practicing songwriting. However, Evelyn is a little different than other musicians. She is deaf. She lost most of her hearing when she was 12 years old. But that didn't stop her from becoming a musician. Evelyn knew she had a special connection to her music. She learned how to listen to music by letting sound waves travel through her body. Evelyn's music is so beautiful that she was invited to play at the opening ceremony of the 2012 Olympics. Evelyn did not let being deaf stop her from doing what she wanted to do. Even though she has a hard job, she is successful at it. She is an inspiration to musicians around the world and to all of us.

Speaking

Talking about the Past

Track 2-22   A.   Page 111

Thirty-five-year-old Alastair Humphreys believes in challenges. For example, he faced many challenges riding his bike 46,000 miles around the world. Many thought he was a professional biker, but he wasn't! In 2011, Humphreys decided to go on small, challenging adventures inside England. He walked along Britain's infamous road, the M25. Alastair swam the Thames, slept out underneath the stars, and spent four days living off the land. Each trip he took was cold and it was challenging. To inspire people, Humphreys made a video of ten challenges. The four-minute video encourages future adventurers to sign up for a race, to do things before and after work, and to pick a place on a map and visit it. Humphreys believes you should not be afraid of a challenge. He believes you should have ambition too! He learned that we can be successful no matter how hard the challenges are.

Lessons A & B

Viewing

Track 2-23   B.   Page 112

Antarctica is large. It is larger than Europe or Australia. It covers over five million square miles. Its thick ice holds 70 percent of the world's fresh water. But it is also known as the world's largest desert because it gets only about two inches of snow a year. It is also the coldest place on Earth. The average temperature is -90 degrees Celsius in winter to above freezing in summer along the coast. Many tourists visit Antarctica in the summer between November and February. They go to see the beautiful frozen land, the icebergs, and animals such as whales and seals. Antarctica is also famous for its many penguins. Antarctica is a land of beauty and challenge for the people who live and work there and for the tourists who visit.

Lesson B

Building Vocabulary

Track 2-24   A. Using a Dictionary   Page 114

activity
environment
equipment
goal
obstacle
realize
sled

Dr. Michael Davis became interested in working with racehorses as a young boy living outside of Houston, Texas. He realized he wanted to become a veterinarian. In high school, he worked for many hours toward that goal without getting paid. Working with horses may have prepared Dr. Davis for his future job—working with sled dogs in Alaska. The sled dogs Dr. Davis works with race in the Iditarod Trail Sled Dog Race. It is a very difficult race across 1,000 miles of Alaska.

Dr. Davis works in a very challenging environment and must overcome many obstacles such as working in extreme cold and dangerous conditions. He has to do his job as a veterinarian in a place which is very far from cities or towns that have good equipment. "The only thing we can count on is what we've brought with us," he says. Dr. Davis loves doing activities outside. He loves his job, even though it is in a very challenging environment.

Using Vocabulary

A: Did you know that astronauts are known as space explorers? It takes them many years of hard work to reach their goal of becoming an astronaut.
B: Yeah! And they have such a cool job! Imagine working in such an extreme environment.
A: They are so brave! Last week I saw a picture of Neil Armstrong as he climbed down the ladder to step on the moon. I realized that being an astronaut is really hard and dangerous.
B: You're right. Astronauts have such a challenging job.
A: They have to be in good physical and mental shape.
B: I went to NASA last year and saw where they performed many activities underwater. The underwater environment is like space.
A: Did they have a lot of special equipment to work with?
B: Yes, they did! While I was at NASA, I discovered that being an astronaut is not an easy job.
A: I agree! I think a person must have a lot of ambition to become an astronaut. I think we can learn from them and not let any obstacles stop us from reaching our goals in life.

Developing Listening Skills

Regular verbs in the simple past tense that end in -*ed* have three different pronunciations. In Lesson **A**, we learned about the /d/ sound. In this section, we will learn about the /t/ and /id/ sounds.

-*ed* has a /t/ sound after these final sounds: /f/, /k/, /p/, /s/, or /sh/

Examples: laugh → laughed → laugh/t/, ask → asked → ask/t/

-*ed* has an /id/ sound after these final sounds: /t/ or /d/

Examples: want → wanted → want/id/, add → added → add/id/

1. helped
2. finished
3. walked
4. looked
5. stopped
6. visited
7. repeated
8. ended
9. decided
10. needed

1. liked
2. wanted
3. looked
4. added
5. wished

Listening: A Conversation

A: Hi! I haven't seen you in a long time! Where have you been?
B: Well, for the past five years I worked as a taxi driver in New York.
A: Really? How did you like it?
B: It was a really tough job! I worked 10 hours a day. So I didn't have much time to see my family or friends.
A: That's hard. How were your customers?
B: Some of my customers were OK, but some were not so nice. And you never knew who would get into your taxi.
A: I see. So what are you doing now?
B: I'm not working now and am thinking of changing jobs. I'm trying to find a less stressful job here in New York. What about you? What have you been doing?
A: Me? Oh, I'm still a chef. Last year, they moved me to one of the most famous restaurants in New York.
B: Good for you! How was it?
A: It was a challenging year! I had to work for many hours in a hot kitchen, plus I had to work really fast!
B: That sounds hard. How were your customers?
A: Well, the customers were demanding and expected the best. I had to provide the freshest and most delicious food possible. Customers also expected the same time after time, and if I made a small mistake with an order, my customers were not happy and neither was my supervisor.
B: Are you still there at the restaurant?
A: Yeah, and I like working there, but I had to adapt to working in a challenging environment really quickly!
B: Wow! You make my job as a taxi driver seem easy!

Exploring Spoken English

1. It takes many years of practice and dedication to learn to play the piano.
2. If you work on oil pipes in Alaska, you often have to work outside in snow and very cold weather.
3. Olympic athletes start practicing at a young age and work for many hours every day, for many years.

A: Hey, Melissa. I read an article in a magazine yesterday. It was about famous businesswomen and how they became successful. Two of the women in the article were Coco Chanel and Estée Lauder. Coco Chanel was a fashion designer and Estée Lauder was famous for her beauty products.

B: That's funny! We must have read the same article! Wasn't the article interesting? I enjoyed reading how the women believed in themselves. They knew they would be successful.
A: Yeah. These women also loved what they did. They worked many hours to succeed. They knew they had good products.
B: True. But they also knew they did not have all the answers and wanted to learn from others. They read journals, books, and magazines. They made many mistakes while building their businesses but they learned from their mistakes.
A: That's right! Even though some people told them they would not succeed, they continued and never gave up. They believed that they needed persistence to be successful.
B: Persistence? What does that mean?
A: If you have persistence it means you continue trying even if something is difficult or challenging.
B: Oh. What I find interesting is that Coco Chanel had a very difficult childhood. She did not have money and had to work very hard. But she never gave up her dream of designing clothes. Estée Lauder also worked hard to learn about beauty products. She learned from her uncle, who had a laboratory and made facial creams.
A: You know, each of these women had a dream. They wanted to build successful businesses. They dreamed of a better future for themselves, and they worked for it. They took risks. They left the comfort of their homes to build their empires.
B: Yeah, I guess that's what it takes to become a successful businessperson.

Track 2-33   A.   Page 119

1. Walt Disney was unsuccessful in many businesses before he started Disneyland.
2. The ice and cold in Alaska make it a difficult environment to work in.
3. Humphreys walked along the M25.
4. Astronauts practice how to work underwater before they go into space.
5. Working as a chef is challenging because you work in hot kitchens for many hours.

Unit 7: Lost and Found
Lesson A

Building Vocabulary

Track 2-34   A. Using a Dictionary   Page 124
capital
century
civilization
emperor
internal
resources
temple
valuable

Track 2-35   C. Meaning from Context   Page 124

What Happened to Angkor Wat?

The kingdom of Angkor Wat was in Cambodia. It lasted from the 9th to the 15th century. Seven hundred fifty thousand people lived in its capital, Angkor. It was the largest city of its time. Angkor was known as a royal city. The kings of Angkor said they were world emperors of Hindu teachings.

They built temples for themselves. People did not use money in Angkor. They used rice instead. Over centuries, the people of Angkor built hundreds of miles of waterways. The civilization learned how to save and use water. Other kingdoms had problems with too little or too much water. This made Angkor's waterways very valuable resources. But over time, the world around Angkor changed. Angkor faced economic and religious challenges. Also, the weather changed. Finally, Angkor's water system, which had worked for 600 years, broke down. This caused internal fighting and the end of an amazing civilization.

Using Vocabulary

Track 2-36   B.   Page 125

A: Do you know where Angkor Wat is?
B: Yes. Angkor Wat is in Cambodia.
A: How long did the kingdom last?
B: It lasted from the 9th to the 15th century.
A: Wow! That's almost 600 years! How many people lived in its capital, Angkor?
B: I think almost 750,000 people lived there.
A: I think it's interesting that the kings called themselves world emperors.
B: They also had many temples made to themselves.
A: Yes, you are right. Something else that is interesting is that they had no money!
B: Right! They used rice instead of money. But what is Angkor famous for?
A: Angkor is famous for its old waterways. They were a very valuable resource.
B: What finally happened to Angkor?
A: Internal fighting ended that amazing civilization.

Developing Listening Skills

Listening: A Guided Tour

Track 2-37   A. Listening for Main Ideas and B. Listening for Details   Page 126

Hi, everyone, and welcome to the British Museum. My name is Sabrina, and today I will be your tour guide. Let me start by giving you some information about the museum. The British Museum is located in the center of London. It opened in 1753, and since that time, millions of visitors have visited the museum to learn more about history and culture. OK . . . so let me introduce you to the room we are standing in. This room is called the Great Court. The Great Court opened in 2000. In the Great Court, you will find information desks to your right and left. If you get hungry or thirsty, there are two coffee shops in the back of the Great Court. In addition, there are four elevators. The restrooms are next to the Reading Room. Finally, in the center is the Round Reading Room. OK . . . any questions? Great! Please follow me as we walk down the corridor to room 52. Everything in this room is about Ancient Persia. Iran's civilization is over 2,500 years old. Cyrus the Great established the first Persian Empire in the 6th century BC. It soon became one of the largest and most powerful kingdoms. In the glass case, in the center of the room, is the Cyrus Cylinder. It was discovered in 1897. As you can see, this cylinder is not very big, but it is very important because of the different laws that are recorded on it. These laws tell us a lot about life in ancient Persia. For example, there were laws that protected people of different religions and cultures so that everyone lived peacefully together. That is why it is often known as the first charter of human rights. If you go to the United Nations in New York, you will see a copy of the Cyrus Cylinder. Now, if you look on your right, you will see . . .

After Listening

Track 2-38 Pronunciation: Word Stress   Page 127

In English, when we say a word, the first syllable is usually louder than the other syllables. This is called *word stress*. Word stress is a very important part of spoken English. There are three rules about word stress:

1. Every word has just one stressed syllable.
2. Most two syllable *nouns* and *adjectives* are stressed on the **first** syllable.

Examples: **A**pril, **an**cient, **ta**ble, **mo**ther, **hap**py, **ye**llow, **ho**tel

3. Many two syllable *verbs* are stressed on the **second** syllable.

Examples: de**cide**, re**peat**, be**gin**

Track 2-39 A.   Page 127

1. temple
2. paper
3. answer
4. people
5. prevent
6. survive
7. quiet
8. explain
9. sleepy
10. perfect

Exploring Spoken English

Track 2-40 E.   Page 130

Were Aztec, Olmec, and Maya Rubber-Making Masters?

Three thousand years ago, ancient civilizations in Mexico and Central America used to make rubber. The Aztec, Olmec, and Maya civilizations used to make rubber from trees and plants. Some of the rubber they made used to bounce. The Mayas used to play a lot of ball games. They made balls for their games with this rubber. In ancient Maya, games used to play an important part in their religion. These ball games were played to show good against evil. Sometimes the games ended in human sacrifice. The losers were beheaded—that means they used to have their heads cut off!

Lesson B

Building Vocabulary

Track 2-41 A. Using a Dictionary   Page 134

artifact
chief
estimate
excavate
gold
native
site
treasure

Track 2-42   C. Meaning from Context   Page 134

The Golden Chiefs of Panama

In 2005, archaeologist Julia Mayo and her team began to excavate a cemetery in Panama. The cemetery was more than 1,000 years old. Many treasures were found at this site. In 2010, she and her team uncovered a powerful warrior chief wearing gold. In 2011, they uncovered another chief. Specialists at the Smithsonian Institution studied what Mayo's team found. They learned something important about this ancient civilization. The native people lived in simple houses, but they were rich and cultured enough to understand fine art.

Mayo thinks the cemetery has about 20 more chiefs like the two she excavated. Because her team of 10 works slowly, in four years they have dug up just two percent of the cemetery. She estimates that if work continues at this speed, the last artifact will be excavated 196 years from now!

Developing Listening Skills

Track 2-43   Listening for Emphasized Words   Page 136

When listening to a conversation or lecture, pay attention to the loudest and slowest words. These emphasized words usually contain important information. Less important words are usually spoken quickly and softly. In a question such as, "Did you *find anything*?" The words *find* and *anything* are stressed or emphasized. In the sentence, "Not long after they started to dig, they found a *warrior* made of *gold*," the words *warrior* and *gold* are emphasized.

Before Listening

Track 2-44   A.   Page 136

Tired of staying home?
Need a **vacation**?
Give us a **call**!
We specialize in **archaeological** tours.
For more information, call **1-800-555-1800**.

Listening: A Conversation

Track 2-45   A. Listening for Details, B. Note-Taking, and C. Checking Predictions   Pages 136–137

A: When you were younger, did you ever look for lost treasure in your backyard?
B: Yeah, I did! I remember when we had just moved into a house with a big backyard. My sister and I went into the backyard and started exploring it. We thought we might find lost gold there.
A: Did you find anything?
B: Yes, as a matter of fact, we did! One of the trees had a small hole in it. The hole was just big enough for my sister to put her hand in. She pulled out a very small box! Inside the box was a ring. I don't think the ring was very valuable. We never had anyone estimate its value.
A: Well, I never found any lost treasure. But I read that some workers in Scotland uncovered some artifacts. They found 120 Roman shoes. The shoes were over 2,000 years old!
B: Really! How did they find them?
A: Well, workers were digging to build a supermarket. They uncovered very old shoes. But that's not all! They started to

excavate some more. They found Roman jewelry, coins, and pottery at the site.

B: Wow! Imagine that. The workers were responsible for uncovering a very wealthy archaeological site. Now that's what you call finding a lost treasure!

Exploring Spoken English

Track 2-46 A. Using a Dictionary   Page 138

Inca Skull Surgeons Were "Highly Skilled"

In Peru, on a site near the ancient Inca capital of Cuzco, archaeologists found very old skulls. These skulls belonged to natives and were more than 2,000 years old. For the archaeologists, these skulls were more valuable than treasures of gold. The skulls showed that Inca surgeons made holes in patients' skulls to treat head injuries. The procedure was usually performed on injured men. These men probably got injured while fighting. In the beginning, the procedure was new. People who had the surgery died. But by the 1400s, Inca surgeons had more experience with the procedure. Archaeologists estimate almost 90 percent survived the surgery. Today, surgeons perform similar procedures on people who have severe head trauma.

Exploring Spoken English

Track 2-47 D. and F. Note-Taking   Page 139

A: Last summer we went to Turkey. We visited an ancient Roman spa city!

B: I'm sorry, could you repeat what you just said? A spa city? What is that?

A: Let me explain. In 1998, archaeologists discovered the ancient spa city of Allianoi.

B: What do you mean? Why did you call it a spa city?

A: Because the city was famous for its bathhouses. Important Romans would visit the city to go to the bathhouses. That is why it is called *The Spa City*.

B: Wow! Are the bathhouses still there?

A: Yes and no.

B: What do you mean by yes and no?

A: Well, they are building a dam near Allianoi. So, to save the bathhouses, Turkish officials decided to rebury the site with sand! They want to save the bathhouses by keeping them buried under sand.

Unit 8: A New View
Lesson A

Building Vocabulary

Track 2-48 A. Meaning from Context   Page 144

1. A device can help some people live an easier life.
2. Robots with artificial intelligence can do many things.
3. Robots can respond to a command given to them.
4. Our brains control how we think and what we do.
5. Our brains communicate to the rest of our body.
6. The brain sends a signal to artificial limbs telling them to move.
7. People without a limb often have difficulties doing everyday activities.
8. Bionic limbs or parts will allow people to live normal lives.

Developing Listening Skills

Track 2-49 Pronunciation: Contractions with *Will*
Page 146

We often use *will* when we talk about the future. In spoken English, *will* is often contracted or made shorter. *Will* becomes *-ll* and is joined to the subject.

I	I'll
He	He'll
She	She'll
It	It'll
We	We'll
They	They'll

Examples:

I will see you tomorrow.	➝ I'll see you tomorrow.
He will give a lecture.	➝ He'll give a lecture.
We will buy a robot.	➝ We'll buy a robot.

Listening: A Scientific Talk

Track 2-50 A. Listening for the Main Idea and B. Listening for Details   Page 147

A: Good afternoon! Today I'll be talking about an interesting topic. But first let me ask you, how many of you have seen Steven Spielberg's movie *Jurassic Park*? If you haven't seen the movie, it is about a scientist who clones extinct dinosaurs and other animals.

B: Excuse me professor, but what do you mean by *clone* and *extinct*?

A: Oh! Let me explain! OK . . . *cloning* means to make a copy of something. Much like what a photocopying machine does. And *extinct* means something that is no longer alive. So, when we talk about cloning dinosaurs, we mean making copies of them!

B: But is that possible? Can scientists really do that? Can scientists clone dinosaurs? If scientists clone dinosaurs, then they'll walk and live on Earth again! What will they eat? Will they come into the cities? Will they eat people? Oh! I don't think it is a good idea to clone dinosaurs!

A: OK, slow down. Scientists now have the tools they need to clone mice. They think they can use the same technique to clone larger animals from the Ice Age.

C: Professor, how long ago was the Ice Age?

A: The last Ice Age was about 20,000 years ago.

C: Do you mean scientists can clone animals from 20,000 years ago?

A: Well, it's possible. We do have the technology, but it is very, very expensive. But let me ask you another question. Do you think it is a good idea to clone animals? If it is OK to clone animals, is it OK to clone humans? I'll let you think about that as I continue my talk . . .

Exploring Spoken English

Track 2-51 A.   Page 148

1. The microphone is small.
2. Robots are helpful.
3. Artificial limbs are difficult to use.
4. The scientist is excited.
5. Dinosaurs are extinct.

Track 2-52 C. Page 150

Robots will think, act, and communicate like humans. Are we ready?

A new group of robots will soon help us in our homes, schools, and offices. According to some robotics professors, in five or 10 years, robots will work in human environments. We will watch and communicate with our robots from our computers at work. Some robots may cook for us, fold the clothes, and babysit our children. They will also take care of our elderly parents.

Here are some good questions many people ask. What will these future robots look like? Will they change the way we communicate with each other? Are we ready for them? Studies show that people want robots to act like humans. But we don't want them to look like humans! And, we don't want them to make mistakes. Engineers and scientists want to make robots that make us happy. They want to make sure they will help us and make us comfortable. In the future, we don't know if everyone will have a robot at home. But we do know that robots will be a part of our future.

Lessons A & B

Viewing

Track 2-53 C. Page 152

Augmented Smart Phones

Imagine putting on a pair of glasses and seeing bubbles floating before your eyes! These bubbles are filled with information about things you see on the street. This is augmented reality. For many people, augmented reality is already here. It is in their smart phones. Some smart phones have a built-in GPS, compass, and camera. Smart phones can help us find nearby banks and restaurants or the closest subway or bus stop. These smart phones also give us information about other points of interest in some cities. With augmented reality, if you point the phone's camera at a restaurant, you'll see reviews about the restaurant on your screen. Augmented reality is a powerful tool that has taken us into the world of tomorrow.

Lesson B

Building Vocabulary

Track 2-54 Meaning from Context Page 154

Future Farms

Architect Blake Kurasek wanted to design special apartments. He called them Living Skyscrapers. These future apartments will be special. People will live in them, but there will also be greenhouses in the building. Vegetables and plants will grow inside the greenhouses. Fruit trees will grow on balconies. The ground floor will have a market. Residents will sell the fruit and vegetables they grow in the market.

Another kind of future farm was designed by Italian architects. They wanted to create farms that use seawater. The farms are called Seawater Vertical Farms. They will be high from the ground and will use water from the sea. The seawater will cool and provide water for greenhouses.

These farms will be used in dry areas and near the sea. They will be used where there is not enough freshwater or enough vegetables.

The Pyramid Farm is another way we will grow food in the future. The Pyramid Farm will look like a big pyramid. It will grow fruits and vegetables. It will also change sewage into energy for the farm.

Developing Listening Skills

Track 2-55 Listening for Statements of Opinion Page 156

When speakers want to give an opinion, they may use the following expressions:

In my opinion . . .
The way I see it . . .
If you want my opinion . . .
I think . . .
As far as I'm concerned . . .

Examples: *In my opinion, growing our own vegetables and selling them in a market is a good idea!*

I think robots will be very helpful around the house.

Listening: A Debate between Friends

Track 2-56 A. Listening for Main Ideas, B. Listening for Details, and C. Checking Predictions Pages 156–157

Jackie: Hey, Angela! I listened to a really interesting program on the radio this morning. It was about apartments of the future. Scientists think we will have the technology to build special apartments. These apartments will have greenhouses where people will grow their own fruits and vegetables.
Angela: Hi, Jackie. I know. I heard it this morning, too. In my opinion, the topic was interesting, but I disagree with what they said.
Jackie: Why? Don't you think it will be possible to grow fruits and vegetables inside apartments?
Angela: Well, not really. I understand scientists and architects want to build special apartments that will have greenhouses in them. They say residents will grow fruits and vegetables in the greenhouses. And, they say residents will sell what they grow in markets. Jackie, as far as I'm concerned, I don't think people will do that!
Jackie: I disagree with you. I think people will want to grow their own food. It will be cheaper. And besides, residents in these apartments will have vegetables and fruits all the time!
Angela: Yes, but people who live in apartments are not farmers! Who is going to have all that time to water the vegetables and fruits? People go to work all day and come home tired. They want to rest—not go into greenhouses and start watering plants!
Jackie: True. But, the way I see it, many things will change in the future. Just think—there will be more people and not enough land. So, we will have to think of new ways to grow our food.
Angela: Well, if you want my honest opinion, I don't think any of this is a good idea. I am happy I am living now and not in the future!

Exploring Spoken English

Track 2-57   A.   Page 158

A: Did you watch TV last night? In the future, people who need a body part are going to get one from labs. Scientists are going to grow body parts from people's cells.

B: What was that again?

A: I said, in the future, scientists are going to grow body parts in the lab!

B: Wow! Really? They are going to grow body parts like ears and eyes in the lab?

A: Yes! Scientists are going to grow body parts that are called bioartificial organs.

B: I guess that will help people who are sick. In the future, if a person needs a heart, liver, or other organ, surgeons will order a bioartificial organ for them!

A: Isn't that amazing? In the future, do you think we are going to live a lot longer than we do today?

B: I don't know. But, I think life is going to be more interesting than it is today!

Unit 1: Coming of Age

Narrator:
Around the world, every child becomes an adult in a different way. Yoro Sisse is a 16-year-old Fulani boy from Diafarabe, Mali. Every year, teams of young Fulani boys, like Yoro, make a long trip. They do this to find food for their cows.

During the dry season, the cows can stay near the Fulani's home. But in the wet season, there is too much rain for the cows to stay there. The boys take their cows into the Sahel, near the Sahara Desert. In the desert there aren't many trees or plants. It is very dry. The boys travel along the edge of the desert, moving from place to place.

The boys' trip can take almost eight months. There is little food for the boys near the desert. They do not carry a lot of food with them. They usually only drink milk.

Yoro:
We have to keep moving to find more food for our cows. Our job is to bring back fat cows.

Narrator:
This is something every Fulani boy has to do. It's a very important job. When Yoro goes home, everyone will look at his cows. If the cows are all OK, the other Fulani people will know Yoro can take good care of his herd. Then, they will say he is not a boy, but a man.

This is Yoro's girlfriend, Aissa. She wants him to come back with good cows because she wants to marry him. In the Fulani tribe, mothers and fathers choose the person their children can marry. If Yoro doesn't come back with good cows, Aissa's parents won't let her marry him.

During the trip, Yoro thinks about many things. He worries about finding food for his cows. He also worries about other people who want to take the cows.

Yoro starts his journey in Diafarabe, Mali. He takes his cows through Mauritania, to the Sahel. The Fulani people have walked this way for thousands of years. Yoro has walked for three months. Now he is going back to his home—and his family, and his girlfriend.

Yoro:
We walk all day without stopping. Sometimes we get very thirsty, and the cows get tired. Often, we don't sleep at night.

Narrator:
The young cows in Yoro's herd look good. Everyone can see Yoro's hard work. He marks them so everyone knows they are his.

The trip is almost over, and Yoro is excited to see his girlfriend.

But now, they still have to cross the river. Yoro swims with his cows. He wants to make sure they are OK.

Across the river, his family and friends wait for the boys. After a long and difficult trip, Yoro's cows are all OK. It's time to celebrate and have fun.

Unit 2: Highlining Yosemite Falls

Dean Potter:
My name's Dean Potter and I live right here in Yosemite Valley. I've been living here 17 years. This line is one of the hardest lines that I've tried to walk. The moving water, the wind—there's a lot of distractions.

Yosemite, it really brings out my creativity. It's such a powerful place, there's some sort of amazing energy going on that fuels me. Late spring, early summer—it's the perfect time for releasing this massive gush of water over the falls.

I have to be totally analytical to rig a line that's not gonna fail. There's a lot of air right here. I don't want to be thinking about line failure or anything. That's why I have this incredible gear, hundred thousand pound shackle, makes me feel warm and fuzzy. This stuff called Amsteel, so it's this soft cable. It's 40 percent stronger than steel, but it floats. A whole new level, man. It's kinda new for slacklining for people to pull lines with the grip hoist, but it's something that tightrope walkers have done probably close to a century.

People just think I'm a lunatic or an adrenaline junkie, and that's not really what's going on with me. The beauty is mostly what I'm concerned with, and that's really why I'm up here trying to cross a line over Yosemite Falls.

I'll just focus on the beauty and on my breath but that water doesn't stop. Like, I wish I had blinders on, something moving so drastically in my field of vision. It's a huge challenge for me.

I'm getting blinded by spray. I'll try one more time and really focus.

Want it. Come on. Let's do it.

I was just being rocked around by the wind and blinded by the spray of the waterfall. Yeah, I was supposed to fall, but somehow I stood back up and kept going.

When I'm out on the line, it really brings out my creativity. And for me, pushing into the unknown is a big part of what I call fun. Seeing a new part of yourself that you didn't know was there. This is when it's fun, right now.

You know if you're lucky, brief moments where you're just seeing everything, seeing the beautiful world, all that's there, right in the moment.

Unit 3: Indian Railways

Narrator:
At the Victoria Terminus in Mumbai, India, it always seems to be rush hour. Every day, approximately two million passengers pass through this train station. The journey to Mumbai is often very stressful, but in this country of over a billion people, the best way to travel is by train.

The British built the railways in India in the 19th century. The first steam train in India was in 1853. Now the Indian Railways travel along 38,000 miles of track.

Many of the trains have impressive names, like the Himalayan Queen and Grand Trunk Express. The Grand Trunk Express has traveled up and down the country since 1929.

Most of India Railways' four billion passengers a year live in big cities, but even rural villages do not usually have to walk for more than a day to get to a station.

With over one and a half million people on its staff, India's railways are the world's largest employer, from the Indian Railways minister down to the key man who makes sure every inch of track is in good condition, the huge workforce keeps this enormous system running.

The railway stations are often an amazing mix of people. There are people selling food, porters carrying bags, and sometimes performance artists.

But the railway is more than just a way to travel. It is like a miniature India. In the second-class carriages, there are people from all over the country from different classes and cultural backgrounds. They talk, play games, and tell stories.

For travelers, the Indian Railways are their own adventure.

Unit 4: Blue Lagoon

Narrator:
It's a giant geothermal lagoon. Essentially a misty lake of hot seawater, it's in a very unusual, very dramatic setting, adjacent to a power plant and surrounded by volcanoes and old lava fields.

This strange and steamy world of black rock and bright blue water is Iceland's most popular attraction. It lures more than three hundred thousand people a year, mostly tourists, but warm water is warm water, and even the locals get into the swim of things.

The blue lagoon looks natural, but it was formed by this geothermal power plant. The plant takes super-heated water out of the ground and uses it to make energy. When they originally pumped it back out into the lava fields, the water formed a lagoon.

According to Grimur Samundsen, it's been a mecca for people looking to soak away their tension ever since.

Grimur Samundsen:
After a strong working weekend, the best thing you can do is go in the water and relax a bit. It's great. It's absolutely great. And afterwards, your skin feels soft, and you feel great and relaxed, and I think that people, you know, they really, really are impressed.

Narrator:
The average temperature in the lagoon is about 100 degrees Fahrenheit. As you swim out toward the center, though, where the main steam vent is, you can feel it getting hotter.

There's blue-green algae in the water and white silica mud on the bottom, which is how the lagoon gets its soft, milky, aquamarine color. But even more unique, they say the water and the mud have curative healing powers, especially for people with skin ailments, like psoriasis.

It looks funny, but a lot of the bathers go over to one corner and slather the wet chalky sediment all over their bodies. Though Iceland may not be thought of as a hot spot for tourists, the Blue Lagoon may yet change some minds.

Unit 5: Pow-Wows

Buck Spotted Tail:
My name is Buck Spotted Tail. I'm from the Rosebud Sioux Reservation in South Dakota. My Indian name is Sinte Gleska. I've been dancing since I've been about six years old, pretty much all my life.

You do one step on one foot, you do on the other foot, and, like, you try to move like the grass. That's pretty much how it was back in the day, and gradually it started changing throughout the years, and the old style was the old style, and they're kind of more put together. The contemporary is more out there and a little more outgoing throughout the song.

It's like a family tradition. It's . . . we watch our families grow up and do the dance, and that's how we gradually grow up and start learning our ways and learning that it's a fun thing that we normally do.

It's a way to bring all our people together in a big celebration, to feed all the people, do a lot of singing, do a lot of dancing, And it has nothing to do with, you know, money or nothing. It's just all of us coming together as all *tiyoŝpayes,* all families coming, you know, all different chiefs' families, you know, all just come have a big *wachipi,* a pow-wow.

Unit 6: Antarctic Challenge

Our plane lands on ice and snow. We are in Antarctica. It is one of the coldest places on Earth. We came here to climb a 2,000-foot rock named Rakekniven. It has taken more than one year of planning, and we are finally here! The Antarctic is a very harsh environment, and we will face many challenges to reach our goal. One of the challenges will be the very cold weather. It is also very windy.

As we load our equipment onto snowmobiles, we think of the 40 miles of snow and ice we will have to cross to get to Rakekniven.

Rakekniven stands in the middle of Queen Maud Land. It stands very tall. We realize it will be a difficult climb. No one has ever climbed the rock before. As we walk towards Rakekniven, we realize how difficult the climb will be.

It will be a very dangerous climb, but we are ready for it. It will be a big accomplishment to climb the rock.

We look at Rakekniven. We know we can climb it. We are ready and have a very skilled team. It is time to begin the climb.

Climbing up the rock is hard because there is no place to put our hands or feet and we must feel our way up.

It is difficult and dangerous. Fear is with us as we climb. One small mistake and we could fall. We could die. The climb is risky. The rock is also very sharp and causes our hands to bleed. Climbing to the top could take days, and we will face many obstacles as we climb up.

This climb is tiring and has put a lot of stress on all of us. But finally, we reach the top! We are extremely happy to be the first team of climbers to ever reach the top of Rakekniven! We pull out our flag to place on top of the rock. What an exciting adventure this has been!

Unit 7: The Lost World of Angkor

Man:
Have you ever been to the ancient city of Angkor in Cambodia?

Woman:
Um, no. No, I haven't.

Man:
Well, that's where we're going today. Angkor used to be the capital of an empire, the Khmer Empire that ruled much of Southeast Asia.

Woman:
Whoa, those are cool buildings!

Man:
I know. Angkor has hundreds of cool buildings. Many of them are temples. Five hundred years ago, it covered more than 600 square kilometers. I mean, it was bigger than Paris! During the 13th century, about 750,000 people were living there.

Woman:
Really?

Man:
Uh huh. Hundreds of years later, in 1860, a French explorer was walking through the jungle and he found the city. He wrote about it and drew pictures. People around the world became interested in Angkor.

Woman:
Wow, look at that face!

Man:
Yeah! The temple of Bayon has more than 200 faces like this carved in stone.

Woman:
And what's this?

Man:
This is the temple of Angkor Wat. The Khmer people built it during the mid-1100s.

Woman:
Wow, it's beautiful.

Man:
You know, hundreds of years ago, there used to be an amazing water system in Angkor. Huge rice fields, thousands of people . . .

Woman:
So what happened?

Man:
Well, no one really knows. In the 12th century, people from Vietnam attacked and burned the city.

Woman:
And did all the people die?

Man:
No, no. The king rebuilt the city and named it Angkor Thom. But then something else happened. The rice fields began to fail.

Woman:
You mean the city didn't get enough rain?

Man:
Yeah, there probably wasn't enough water to grow rice. People stopped building temples, and they began to move away. Over the years, the jungle grew over the buildings, like this temple, called Ta Prohm.

Woman:
Wow, it really looks like a lost city in the jungle.

Unit 8: Augmented Reality

Narrator:
On the campus of New York's university, researchers are looking into the future. It's part of a program designed to change the way we see the world. Professor Steve Feiner and his group of computer science students are working to augment, or increase, reality. This means that they are trying to build up a virtual world that we can integrate, or bring together, with the physical world. This virtual world can give us extra information about what we see and hear. The head-worn device puts text and graphics over a person's normal field of vision. Sophisticated tracking devices allow the computer to constantly update the information on display. Everything is measured exactly where they are. The system allows users to see three-dimensional graphics and images, mapping their location within their surroundings. This is very good for people going into an environment that they do not know much about. Imagine giving firefighters a clear view of building blueprints, even if they cannot see because of the smoke or fire. Or providing pilots with information on the windscreen of their cockpits. Using a global positioning system, or GPS, Feiner's research team is among the first to take augmented reality technology outdoors and into the real world. It can change tourists' experiences! They can learn about the history of a place by looking at the site.

Professor Steve Feiner:
They would see the main asylum building overlaid as sort of a ghost image, on top of their view of Low library. And they could actually walk around that building and look at it and see additional information about it on the handheld.

Narrator:
All of this is very educational, but part of the reason why Feiner wants this to be successful is because he gets lost easily. Having this kind of technology will help him and many others like him. Imagine, if he's successful, you might never get lost again!

CPSIA information can be obtained
at www.ICGtesting.com
Printed in the USA
FFOW03n0859160913
1795FF